MW01038733

CULTURE SHOCK!

A Survival Guide to Customs and Etiquette

KOREA

John Bocskay

Marshall Cavendish
Editions

© 2017 John Nicholas Bocskay

Published by Marshall Cavendish Editions
An imprint of Marshall Cavendish International

Reprinted 2018

A member of the
Times Publishing Group

Other Marshall Cavendish Offices:
Marshall Cavendish Corporation. 99 White Plains Road, Tarrytown NY 10591-9001, USA • Marshall Cavendish International (Thailand) Co Ltd. 253 Asoke, 12th Flr, Sukhumvit 21 Road, Klongtoey Nua, Wattana, Bangkok 10110, Thailand • Marshall Cavendish (Malaysia) Sdn Bhd, Times Subang, Lot 46, Subang Hi-Tech Industrial Park, Batu Tiga, 40000 Shah Alam, Selangor Darul Ehsan, Malaysia

Marshall Cavendish is a registered trademark of Times Publishing Limited

National Library Board, Singapore Cataloguing-in-Publication Data

Name(s): Bocskay, John.
Title: CultureShock! Korea : a survival guide to customs and etiquette / John Bocskay.
Other title(s): Korea : a survival guide to customs and etiquette | Culture shock Korea
Description: Singapore : Marshall Cavendish Editions, [2017] | Series: Culture shock!
Identifier(s): OCN 982086311 | ISBN 978-981-4771-13-9 (paperback)
Subject(s): LCSH: Etiquette—Korea (South). | Korea (South)--Social life and customs. | Korea (South)--Description and travel.
Classification: DDC 951.95--dc23

Printed in Singapore by Markono Print Media Pte Ltd

Photo Credits:
All photos by the author except pages 31, 119, 167 & 245 (Adam Parsons); 25, 30, 157, 196, 198 & 210-211 (Chris Cusick); 151, 162, 199 & 202 (Max Neivandt); 26, 156, 193, 212 & 219 (Mike Dixon); 200-201 & 214 (Ryan Bentley); vi, viii, 7, 8, 10, 19, 34, 60, 64, 69, 72, 208 (Thomas L Coyner); and 100, 112, 130, 160, 191 (Will Jackson). Cover Photo by Shuvra Mondal

All illustrations by TRIGG

ABOUT THE SERIES

Culture shock is a state of disorientation that can come over anyone who has been thrust into unknown surroundings, away from one's comfort zone. *CultureShock!* is a series of trusted and reputed guides which has, for decades, been helping expatriates and long-term visitors to cushion the impact of culture shock whenever they move to a new country.

Written by people who have lived in the country and experienced culture shock themselves, the authors share all the information necessary for anyone to cope with these feelings of disorientation more effectively. The guides are written in a style that is easy to read and covers a range of topics that will arm readers with enough advice, hints and tips to make their lives as normal as possible again.

Each book is structured in the same manner. It begins with the first impressions that visitors will have of that city or country. To understand a culture, one must first understand the people—where they came from, who they are, the values and traditions they live by, as well as their customs and etiquette. This is covered in the first half of the book.

Then on with the practical aspects—how to settle in with the greatest of ease. Authors walk readers through how to find accommodation, get the utilities and telecommunications up and running, enrol the children in school and keep in the pink of health. But that's not all. Once the essentials are out of the way, venture out and try the food, enjoy more of the culture and travel to other areas. Then be immersed in the language of the country before discovering more about the business side of things.

To round off, snippets of information are offered before readers are 'tested' on customs and etiquette. Useful words and phrases, a comprehensive resource guide and list of books for further research are also included for easy reference.

CONTENTS

Dongdaemun Design Plaza, Seoul.

ACKNOWLEDGEMENTS

In writing this book, I was very fortunate to be able to enlist the help of various people, and the resulting work has benefitted enormously from their insight, experience, advice and feedback. Whatever flaws and shortcomings remain are mine alone.

I would like to express my humble and heartfelt thanks to the following people, in no particular order: Kenneth May, Earl Reid, Thomas Locke, George Baca, Jeong Jeong-soon, Kang Young-hee, Eo Hae-jeong, Kim Seon-I, Tom Coyner, Shannon Sawicki, Jen Lee, James Strohmaier, David Balcanquel, Mike Dixon, Yujin Lee, Chris Cusick, Jeff Liebsch, Michael Meyers, Eric Price, CedarBough Saeji, Shuvra Mondal, Minhee Kim-Tharp, Jeff Harrison, Christie Swain, Kwon Seon-ae, Ben May, Krissi Faith, Joe Rawnsley, Robert Perchan, Chris Birdsong, Matthew Sidgreaves, Robert Holley, Joshua Weaver, Will Jackson, Park Jihyun, Peter Underwood, Adam Parsons, Max Neivandt, Katie Mae Klemsen Yee, Ryan Bentley, Bobby McGill and Steve Feldman. Special thanks go to my editor, Shereen Wong, for her sterling guidance from start to finish. My deepest thanks go to my wife Aeran, and my three daughters, Cheyoon, Cheyoung and Chewon, for being my most patient, dependable and charming guides to the country of their birth.

Much of what appears in the pages that follow is also the indirect product of countless interactions over the nearly two decades I've lived in South Korea. To that anonymous legion of friends, students, teachers, acquaintances, colleagues, drinking buddies, good Samaritans and fellow travellers who have enhanced my understanding and eased my acclimation to my adopted home, I bow in gratitude.

Girls wearing traditional *hanbok* (Korean dress) set up for a selfie.

PREFACE

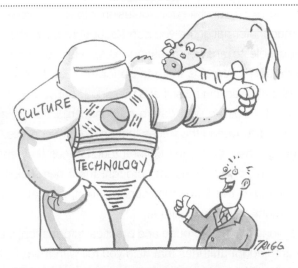

As a high-tech democracy steeped in thousands of years of tradition, South Korea at once presents visitors with much that is familiar, and much that is very different. Novel sights, sounds, tastes, and experiences excite the short-term traveller, but the same novelty can bedevil the long-term resident, who finds that simple tasks once taken for granted—taking a bus, paying a phone bill, knowing how to greet someone—are suddenly complicated.

This pervasive feeling that one is out of step with the norms of the people around you is what is commonly referred to as culture shock, and it can have negative effects on your social relationships, your peace of mind, even your health. Culture shock is one of the prime reasons many expat assignments head home early and perhaps worse, is a big reason why many who stick it out remain grumpy, frustrated and out of sorts, in some cases for years.

The good news is that culture shock is eminently treatable, and many long-term visitors pass through it and come to have rewarding and enjoyable lives in their new home. One of the keys to minimising the confusion is to arm yourself with as much information as you can about your new environs. Being able to answer questions like, "How do I find an apartment?", "What is there to do for fun?" and "How do I avoid embarrassing myself at a meeting?" get you on a firm footing for dealing with day-to-day concerns. To dig a bit deeper, discovering the values that animate the people, the language they speak, the cultural touchstones they share, and the historical forces that brought them here helps the visitor make the leap from survival to appreciation and enjoyment of the new culture.

Beyond this background and practical information, it also helps to adopt attitudes that help you roll with the punches on the bad days, and to draw the most from the good days as you expand your cultural boundaries and the horizons of your world. The question becomes not so much *what* you are looking at, but *how* you choose to see it, the answer to which will have an outsize influence on the quality of your experience in your new surroundings.

In writing this book, I have tried to provide the information, insight and background you need not only to live but to appreciate and enjoy your time in South Korea, whether you are a businessperson, teacher, engineer, missionary, soldier, student, or informed traveller. In doing so, I have drawn on what I have learned about both South Korea itself, and about living and working in South Korea, from the point of view of someone who has called it home for the past eighteen years. Because no one person can know all there is to know about a country—particularly one as dynamic as South Korea—I have been pleased and fortunate to draw on the knowledge and insights of my Korean friends, family, colleagues, teachers and students, as well as the experience and wisdom of other long-term foreign residents who call South Korea home.

To be sure, the descriptions that follow will not apply to every person you meet, nor will your experiences always jibe with everything presented here; indeed, Koreans themselves disagree over how best to characterise their society as it embraces global currents of social and cultural change while striving to preserve a distinctly Korean character. For the better part of the last century, South Korea has transformed in ways that have rendered it all but unrecognisable from one generation to the next—from an impoverished agrarian backwater to a global exporter of technology, culture and style—while new currents continue to drive the process ever forward.

In selecting the material for this book, I have tried to focus on the South Korea that greets the visitor today and to tease out the broad trends, tendencies and undercurrents that are both noticeable and useful for the newcomer to understand, and have strived to illuminate the historical threads and cultural strands that have intermingled to form the modern Korean tapestry, in the hope that the reader be well equipped to both reckon with the present, and to navigate new trends, information and developments as they unfold. It is my sincere wish that this book serve you well in softening your landing in Korea, and if you are drawn in deeper, that it provide you a springboard to continued discovery.

MAP OF SOUTH KOREA

CHINA

NORTH
KOREA

KOREA BAY

EAST SEA

• SEOUL

SOUTH
KOREA

YELLOW SEA

KOREA STRAIT

JAPAN

JEJU STRAIT

JEJU ISLAND

FIRST
IMPRESSIONS

> ❮No man ever steps in the same river twice; for it is not the same river, and he is not the same man.❯

— Heraclitus

My earliest impression of Korea came in a 1998 phone call. I was a recent college graduate with an itch to work abroad, and was sending out resumes to anywhere for anything at all. Had things worked out differently, I might have been a house-sitter in the Canary Islands, or a newsletter editor in St. Kitts and Nevis—wherever that was—but it was an English teaching franchise in South Korea who was the first to reply to my queries. A telephone interview was arranged, and the next day I found myself on the phone with their recruiter.

"If there's some kind of cultural misunderstanding in the classroom, how would you handle it?" he asked me, and I lost my footing right out of the gate. I had grown up in a 99 per cent white suburb of New York City, where the most serious cultural misunderstanding I had ever witnessed in a classroom was when my 9th grade Social Studies teacher referred to Bon Jovi as "heavy metal". The idea that there could be a truly disruptive gulf between teacher and student had simply never crossed my mind. Fumbling for a coherent answer, I tried to at least assure him that while there was admittedly a lot I didn't understand about Korea (a gross understatement), the bottom line was that I would do my best to identify the source of the misunderstanding, so as to avoid it in the future.

Just as I was beginning to worry that I was already blowing it, he asked me his second question, which turned out to be the last, and for which I had a ready answer.

"Can you be on a plane to Korea in two weeks?"

BBALI BBALI!

In that brief interview, I got my first glimpse of some of the qualities that makes South Korea what it is. For one thing, these were people who made things happen fast, an impression that was only reinforced when I arrived in Seoul exactly two weeks later. Thoroughly jet-lagged after a full day of travel, I was picked up at Gimpo airport and driven straight to the head office for a round of introductions, a cup of coffee and a one-hour crash course in Korean, before being shuttled right back to Gimpo for the hop to Ulsan. There, after dropping my luggage at what was to be my new home, I was whisked to my assigned *hagwon* (institute), where I was instructed to observe one of the outgoing teacher's classes. One hour later, having graduated from my "teacher training", I was thrust into my own classroom, textbook in hand, to teach my first class, all of which took place before I had a chance to sleep, shower, change clothes or simply stop moving for a few minutes. In true Korean fashion, I had hit the ground, not running, but sprinting.

It thus seemed fitting that one of the first phrases I learned in Korean was "bbali bbali", which literally means "quickly, quickly", and I soon began to hear it everywhere. "Little" Ulsan (population one million) had a palpable buzz that made even New York (which bills itself as "the city that never sleeps") seem drowsy in comparison. Everyone in Ulsan was doing something, going somewhere, driving just a touch too fast and setting deadlines that would often seem to pass before you had known about them. Korea is the only place where I have ever felt obliged to walk *up* a moving escalator, lest I be considered lazy or become an obstacle to dozens of other people clambering up behind me. Even hospital patients seemed unable to sit still, and could often be seen shuffling around town in their gowns and slippers, a rolling IV stand in one hand and a cigarette in the other, on their way to God-knows-where. "Bbali bbali" seemed to be the motto of South Korea, and the subsequent years have done little to alter that initial impression.

This sense of urgency was also apparent in the rate at which they were building up their cities. The first clue was the towering cranes that sprouted everywhere, and the apartment blocks that seemingly rose before my eyes, in some cases creating entire neighbourhoods—replete with schools, supermarkets and dozens of real estate agencies—

where only a field had been before. Older buildings were demolished and replaced so quickly that it occasionally affected your ability to give directions, as the hair shop you had used as a landmark last week was now a Dunkin Donuts. That I arrived during the Asian Economic Crisis, which hit Korea hard and required a bailout from the International Monetary Fund, made this rapid buildup all the more striking. Far from resembling the economic train wreck I was reading about in the papers, the country before me seemed to be humming along—the mobile hospital patient writ large.

The longer I stayed, the more apparent was the remarkable scale of construction. An incomplete list of what has been built in Busan since I moved here includes two suspension bridges, three subway lines (and another currently under construction at this writing), a World Cup soccer stadium, the world's largest department store, eight of the ten tallest buildings in Korea (six of which are among the 30 tallest residential buildings in the world) and enough high rise apartments to house several armies and their next of kin. The university where I now work has added a soccer field, baseball field and two multi-storey buildings, while the neighbourhood around us has acquired a mall and cinema, countless restaurants and coffee shops and an apartment complex where an army base used to be. A recently-retired professor I know remembers when the entire area was a melon farm.

One of the things I noticed straight away was that for a country that claims thousands of years of history, I had to go out of my way to find any structure that had been built more than thirty or forty years ago. Compared to European cities of comparable age, there is relatively little architectural trace of the millennia that have passed in Korea, and one does tend to have to look for it. Except for defensive walls and city gates, nearly everything built before the twentieth century was made of wood, which, in addition to being susceptible to natural decay, has often been put to the torch during the many invasions and wars that have visited the peninsula throughout its history right down to the 20th century. Nearly every temple I visited was a reconstruction of a much older one that had been destroyed in an invasion centuries ago. I would also learn that many more of the old buildings were razed in Korea's rush to modernise, when neighbourhoods of densely packed, single-story *hanok* houses were levelled to make way for the massive apartment blocks that were springing up everywhere. Now that the dust of occupation, war and industrialisation has settled, the Korea that greets the visitor today can boast of only a fraction of what stood here before, while much of the traditional architecture that remains struggles to hang on in the face of ever-encroaching and powerful developmental forces.

As a result of the race to get a rapidly growing urban population properly housed, it seemed that things like right angles and strict adherence to building codes were considered optional, and the cities had a rough-around-the-

"Biwon ("secret garden"), set behind Seoul's Changdeok Palace, was once the private garden of the royal families of the Joseon Dynasty (1392–1910). Today it is open to the public and is a popular tourist attraction year round."

edges look and feel. Ill-placed paving stones tripped me on the sidewalk, improperly sized windows and doors often stuck or rattled in their frames and handymen rather unnervingly employed duct tape in a far wider range of applications than the manufacturer clearly intended. As someone who had been hired as a teacher with no experience, this willingness to make do had certainly worked in my favour and tempered the urge to complain, but it was never reassuring to realise that the only thing standing between you and calamity was sometimes just a few inches of tape, a length of knotted twine or a bungee cord.

A common sight in Korea, in its constant rush toward urban development.

Despite all that, everything seemed to work, and if it didn't, it was repaired or replaced with similar speed, which is still true today. Last year, a ten-metre section of water main in the alley leading to my house was excavated and replaced, and the whole alley repaved, all between the time I left for work and the time I arrived home. Korea is also the place to be if you ever have a problem with a product, as taking a broken phone or appliance to a service centre almost always results in a quick, cheap repair, or in some cases, replacement of the defective item with a new one.

The changes in construction between then and now have been dramatic in terms of materials, design and guiding principles. As the urgency to house its swelling urban population subsided and the downsides of hasty construction became apparent, speed gave way first to style, then to livability, the current buzzword of urban development plans from Seoul to Jejudo. As drab concrete gives way to steel and glass, the new arrival is more apt to complain of too much light in his apartment than not enough (if he must complain about something). The cookie cutter apartments of the 1980s and 1990s still populate the cityscapes, but newer buildings are apt to have more idiosyncratic designs. Even my point of entry, Gimpo Airport, has been brushed aside and relegated to domestic duties by Incheon International Airport, an airy glass-and-steel complex that regularly wins annual Best Airport awards for its design, efficiency and numerous amenities, which include a cinema, a golf course, a culture museum, a spa (with sleeping rooms) and an ice rink.

LAND OF THE MORNING *WHAT?*

In the 1880s, the American businessman and astronomer Percival Lowell travelled around Korea and later published a book about his experience and reflections, in which he dubbed Korea "The Land of The Morning Calm". This nickname still occasionally appears in the type of tourist literature that seeks to brand Korea as a land of twirling women in colourful *hanbok* singing *Arirang* in pristine green valleys, but one of the first questions foreigners ask on hearing this sobriquet is, "To what country can this 'morning calm' possibly refer?" While Korea certainly may have been laconic in Lowell's time, one no longer gets the sense that "the morning seems to tarry till the middle of the day", as he wrote. The sight of millions of students, workers, shoppers and walkers on the move has more often inspired foreign wags to rebrand Korea as "The Land of the Morning Clamor".

One of the first things that struck me when I first came here was the decibel level—it often seemed as if the whole country was bellowing for your attention. On my very first morning in Korea, I was jolted out of bed at some ungodly hour by what I thought must surely be a public emergency broadcast warning of an incoming North Korean missile, but turned out

The Korea of today is not quite the land of twirling women in colourful *hanbok* anymore.

to be a vendor parked just below my window, blaring a looped recording through loudspeakers mounted on the top of the truck: "Get your dried squid! Three for 5,000 won!" Nearly everywhere I went, retailers blasted music into the streets, creating a cacophony in the densely packed commercial districts. If a new business opened, they cranked the amps to eleven: more than once I approached what sounded like an outdoor rave only to find two young women shouting into a microphone on an empty street to announce the grand opening of an electronics store.

Even the Buddhist monks, ensconced in their serene mountain temples, seemed to be in on it: rising before dawn, breathing deeply of the misty, mountain air and repeatedly swinging a log suspended on chains into an iron bell the size of a Volkswagen. A monk once explained to me that this was a symbolic call for the whole world to awake, though I must admit it has always seemed fairly literal to me.

The Gwangan Bridge lit up on a weekday night.

Korea was bright as well, and neon was everywhere: on the shop signs, the crosses of church steeples and the edges of motels—there was even a popular style of children's shoes with lights in the heel that flashed with each footfall and were accompanied by a squeak sound effect, just in case your toddler was not already making quite enough noise. While recent laws and ordinances have muffled some of the worst noise polluters, the Korean love of lights has shown few signs of abating. If ever I am in danger of forgetting this, the view from Busan's Gwanganli Beach, just a short walk from my house, serves as a good reminder. Since 2003, our horizon has been dominated by the Gwangan Bridge, which in addition to its primary role as an elevated roadway, pulls extra duty as the launching pad of Busan's annual fireworks displays, as well as the host of a nightly light show, in which tens of thousands of synchronised LED lights installed on the bridge's cables and supports make horses, seagulls and hearts appear to race from end to end, choreographed to the bouncy strains of Jacques Offenbach's "Can Can", because why not.

GO HARD OR GO HOME

Then and now, Koreans have displayed a gung-ho attitude in their approach to everything from work to study to play. I saw people everywhere working hard, or at least making a very good show of it, and as they made clear during my whirlwind arrival, they expected me to work hard too. There was a sense that not knowing exactly what you were doing was no excuse not to do a good job, and they apparently assumed that you'd eventually figure out what you needed to do (which I did).

I also soon learned that one had to be very ill indeed to take a sick day; it was far more common to see feverish colleagues and students don a surgical mask, drag themselves in and park their heads on their desks. And the same was apparently expected of me. The one day a nasty bout of food poisoning forced me to call in sick, the head teacher's persistence in asking about the nature of my illness and whether I was "totally sure" that I couldn't come in finally obliged me to clarify the precise nature of my "accident" on the way to work.

"A-ha," she said, "I think you should probably stay home."

Prior to arrival, I had heard talk of the legendary Korean emphasis on education, but once I was in the trenches it struck me like something closer to a craze, particularly as it applied to the study of English, which almost everyone I met believed was the golden ticket to future success, and was the

reason they were flying thousands of young Westerners like me halfway around the world. Many of the elementary school students at our academy finished at 10pm, often after they had already attended two or three other academies for math, art, science, taekwondo or music, and those who finished earlier were merely off to their next institute class.

While most of them seemed to bear the weight of school as a heavy burden, most displayed no outward sign of rebellion and seemed resigned to long days as their lot. I was surprised to find others, however, who took obvious pleasure in studying, and I was many times struck by how even students as young as nine years old could see school not as a necessary evil but as something of both pragmatic and intrinsic value, a surprisingly mature attitude that had taken me considerably longer to acquire.

The gung-ho attitude of Koreans extended even to leisure pursuits, and I got a definite sense that they believed there wasn't much point in doing anything unless you were willing to do it one hundred per cent. Groups of hikers would gear up for Everest only to trot up some local hill. Kids went to the pool not to perfect their cannonballs but to learn the butterfly stroke. PC games were not merely a pastime but a televised "e-sport", and teenagers with nicknames like "SlayerS_Boxer" earned tidy sums tutoring salarymen in the finer points of Starcraft battle tactics.

Even socialising seemed to require some effort, as a night out took us to many different stops, from restaurant to pub to a *noraebang* ("singing room"), where even the shyest member of the group was emboldened to belt out the high notes in Steelheart's "She's Gone" or die trying. Meals were bountiful and "excessive drinking" did not appear to be an operational concept, as the only observable limits to our nights on the sauce with Korean friends and colleagues were imposed more often by gravity and consciousness (or lack thereof), than by shame or taboo. Though the following is a fitting description of the Korean ethos more generally, Confucius could just as well have been describing the Korean attitude toward alcohol consumption in particular when he wrote that, "Our greatest glory is not in never falling, but in rising every time we do."

HELLO! NICE TO MEET YOU!

Koreans have always struck me as curious about the foreigners in their midst; in the early days it was virtually impossible to walk down the street without attracting some kind of attention. Middle-aged folks would strike up a conversation in buses, elevators, taxis and steam rooms, and ask me where I was from, if I was married, and why I wasn't married. Groups of schoolchildren would shout, "Hello! Nice to meet you!" from across the street before dissolving into a fit of giggles. Stares were common from young and old; even infants would lock eyes with me, and one could imagine them thinking, "There's just something different about this guy…"

Outside of the capital, foreigners were more of a novelty then, and were only more so the further back one rolls the clock. Visitors to Korea in the 1960s and 1970s talk of being followed around by kids and having their arm hair plucked out by curious grandmothers at the local market.

Or consider the experience of Hendrick Hamel, a Dutch merchant who was shipwrecked in Korea in 1653 and was among the earliest Westerners to arrive on Korea's shores. Though his treatment at the hands of his hosts was far more extreme than long-time expats have encountered in our own time, Hamel's account never fails to resonate, even if faintly, across the centuries: "We were daily invited to appear before several great men, because both the men and their wives as well as their children were curious to see us because the rumour had been spread that we looked more like monsters than like human creatures… In the beginning we couldn't show ourselves on the street or a crowd was following us, or people were surrounding us and were gaping at us… It came thus far that on a certain night the mob broke into our bedrooms in order to drag us, against our will, outside and made fun out of us. We lodged a complaint to our commander about this. He forbade anybody to harass us in any way. From that moment on we could move around freely, without causing the gathering of a crowd."

While the days of feeling like a Martian or a Beatle are gone, Koreans retain a general curiosity about foreign people and cultures, and are much more open to the world than Mr Hamel could have dreamed possible. Even fifteen years ago, it was rare to meet a Korean who wasn't a sailor, soldier or businessman who had been anywhere more distant than

Jejudo, an island to the south of the mainland that was a favourite honeymoon destination for Korean newlyweds. Now, Korean families hit the beaches of Southeast Asia with their kids, university students strap on backpacks and ride the rails in Europe and today's honeymooner is more likely to head to Saipan, Santorini or Sydney than Seogwipo. In the past couple of decades, foreign food trends have swept the country one after the other, such that these days you can't swing a cat downtown without hitting a shop that can pull off a competent carbonara, curry or café latte. Strangers now ask me, "Where are you from?"—a subtle shift from the days when the default assumption was that all foreigners were American (much to the chagrin of my British and Canadian friends). In recent decades, as business, education, travel and large international events like the Olympics and the FIFA World Cup have brought more of us to these shores, Koreans are much more used to having us around.

I was struck then and now by the friendliness shown to me by strangers, and have often felt that as a foreigner I was the beneficiary of kindness that at times seemed to exceed the kindness they might have shown even to another Korean. On my very first night on the town in Seoul, my roommate and I, having forgotten the alley in which our cheap guesthouse was hidden, were escorted there in the wee hours by a passerby who walked ten minutes out of his way in a snowstorm to find a place he had never heard of and deliver us to the door. I could be wrong, but it was hard to imagine him doing the same for any old couple of stumbling idiots.

FIRST IMPRESSIONS

First impressions of Korea tend to be mixed and can vary widely from person to person, setting to setting and year to year, to the point where conversations on this subject will often leave you wondering if you are talking about the same country. Straight off the bat, Korea presents the new arrival with a seemingly never-ending series of paradoxes that defy easy explanation, many of them seemingly both valid and contradictory: Korea is fast; Korea is slow. It's a country mired in the past; it's a country racing headlong into the future. The people are thoughtful and warm; the people are pushy and inconsiderate. They do everything by the book; they do whatever the hell they want. Whenever I thought I had stumbled on a solid formulation of "the real Korea", it was always soon followed by a wealth of counterexamples that sent me back to the drawing board.

I saw, for example, a country that was extraordinarily proud of its achievements, culture and natural scenery—even its very climate, as if the Korean peninsula had been uniquely endowed with seasonal temperature variations and the people themselves had had a hand in it. Yet alongside this pride I sensed insecurity—a sense that despite having pulled off a historic political and economic turnaround, Koreans seemed to feel they hadn't quite made it to the Big Time. This insecurity was often exposed whenever I was asked where I was from. Telling someone that I was from New York, a place that has long been a destination for Korean immigrants, almost always flattered the listener, yet it often lent their next question—"Why did you come to Korea?"—a tone that made it perfectly clear that anyone who left a place like that to come to a place like Ulsan apparently had some explaining to do.

Part of the challenge in characterising Korea lies in the inherent difficulty of describing any country in broad strokes, an undertaking that is perhaps more tempting and more problematic in Korea, where ethnic homogeneity often serves to mask the same broad range of characters that one finds anywhere: the free spirit and the fuddy-duddy, the workaholic and the slacker, the conformist and the rebel, the hipster and the nerd, the straight arrow and the Bacchanalian.

Another challenge is related not to person or place, but to time. Like all countries that have jumped on the development train, South Korea is a perpetual work-in-progress (After all, what "developed" country stops developing?), with customs, habits and lifestyle forever evolving in tandem with technological change, demographic shifts, social transformations and economic vicissitudes. However, unlike almost every other country, Korea's development has been swift, recent and radical, such that one's impression of the country and the people is very much a function of the year one arrived. "No man ever steps into the same river twice,"

Decked-out supporter of the Korean national football team during the 2002 FIFA World Cup.

said the Greek philosopher, Heraclitus, whose words aptly describe the impressions of the repeat visitor to Korea, who, after an interval of many years, returns to find little that he recognises, as the old waters are every moment replaced by the new. Though something one may call "the Korean character" runs as a perceptible undercurrent in this rushing river, this too, as we shall see, moves with the flow. Like Heraclitus's river, the only reliable constant is change.

The last five decades of rapid transformation also helps to make sense of many of the apparent contradictions in the norms and sensibilities we label as typically "Korean". Every generation is a product of its times, as our parents and grandparents are fond of reminding us in lectures that usually began with "Well, in *my* day…" and the same is true of Korea, though the rapid transformation of the country has made the inevitable generation gaps more intense than they otherwise might have been. Consider: today's 75-year-old was born into a Japanese colony and raised by parents who were likely to be poor farmers. The 50-year-olds were born into a country ruled by a Korean military dictatorship that was hell-bent on building an industrial society and were working their fingers to the bone. Their children, today's 25-year-olds, have known nothing but democracy, peace and relative affluence, enjoy a better-than average chance at a university education and have cutting-edge technology at their fingertips. While they all share a language and many other cultural touchstones, all were born into vastly different societies with different concerns, and each was instilled with values and habits appropriate to their times, while shedding those that were out of step. A common trope says that there is an "Old Korea" and a "New Korea" and that they exist "side by side", and while this contains an important germ of truth, it really only hints at a more complex reality: there are not two but many Koreas, and as new streams enter and diverge from the main currents, there are new Koreas being born all the time.

TWO KOREAS?

Despite the difficulty of describing Korea in terms of opposites, there is nonetheless one sense in which Korea has roughly conformed to a binary split—the Korea of people you know, and the Korea of strangers—and it is this dichotomy that I suspect accounts for many of the contradictory impressions, and which lies at the heart of the love/hate relationship some expats experience.

People in the street have often struck me as indifferent or oblivious to the people around them: bumping into others without an acknowledgement or a word, blocking aisles and doorways to stop and stare at a phone or chat as if no one else would dream of using the same door, and in general treating the people around them as if they weren't there. There are of course exceptions, and a relatively tiny number who are genuinely mean or callous, but there was (and is) a perceptible feeling of social invisibility or irrelevance around people I did not know.

However, among those with whom I had any kind of relationship—friends, co-workers, bosses and the staff at my regular haunts—the contrast could not have been more stark, as they treated me with respect and consideration that was at times extraordinary: paying keen attention to my mood, helping me to solve problems and get things done (sometimes at great inconvenience to themselves), trying very hard to ensure that I was comfortable in my new surroundings, behaving like paragons of manners and generosity at the dinner table when we went out to eat and a thousand other acts of kindness, consideration, loyalty and generosity that have only deepened as the years go by.

Unfortunately, the new arrival knows few or no locals, so it is the rough-and-tumble Korea of strangers that strikes the foreign visitor straight away, which, to my mind, is probably one of the reasons that relatively few people (myself very much included) fall in love with Korea at first blush. This is not to say that Koreans are not fond of travellers in their midst. "Is it not a pleasure when friends visit from distant places?" said Confucius, whose aphorisms have enjoined countless generations of Koreans to be agreeable and benevolent hosts, as many foreign travellers will attest.

But if Korea is fond of the traveller, it privileges the long-term resident: the person who stays, digs in, forms relationships and commits for the long haul. Many foreign residents do end up developing a deep and abiding affection for Korea, and over the years, I've had the pleasure of meeting hundreds of foreigners who have lived here quite happily for anywhere from several months to several decades. In almost every case (including my own), their affection for Korea—as with any true friendship—is the product of time invested, relationships forged, commitments made and kept and goodwill offered and received. I've also known many others who have moved on from Korea and found themselves missing it, sometimes to their surprise, and it is precisely these personal bonds that they often cite as the object of their longing. You may still grumble occasionally, as I do, about being momentarily inconvenienced by the indifference of a stranger; but as time goes by, it is the other side of that equation, the Korea of the in-group, that wraps its arms around you and doesn't easily let go.

CHAPTER 2

GEOGRAPHY AND HISTORY

> ❝To grasp "modern" Korea we will first need a tour through previous centuries, to make the point that you may forget about history, but history will not forget about you.❞

— **Bruce Cumings**

THE LAY OF THE LAND

South Korea occupies the southern half of a peninsula that juts out from the eastern edge of the Asian mainland. To the West across the Yellow Sea is China, while Japan lies to the east across the sea that bears its name to everyone except Koreans, who call it the East Sea. To the north is the Democratic People's Republic of Korea (aka North Korea), with whom they share their only land border, the heavily-fortified oxymoron known as the Demilitarized Zone. The southern and western coasts are studded with hundreds of islands, many of them populated, and the largest of which is Jejudo, the product of Mount Halla, a now dormant volcano that rises from the centre and is the tallest peak in the country.

History is partly a product of geography, and perhaps nowhere has this been more apparent than in Korea, where geography has been both a curse and a blessing for thousands of years. Korea lies just close enough to China to have long placed it squarely within China's cultural and political orbit, which has alternately been both a boon and a liability to the Korean people. Yet Korea lies just far enough away from China that total absorption of the peninsula has eluded the Chinese for millennia, and has granted sufficient breathing room for a unique culture and people to emerge, to persist and to ultimately thrive.

Korea's topography can also reward the early-morning hiker or shutterbug.

Korea's placement between China and Japan has facilitated the exchange of goods and ideas in times of relative peace, but has also guaranteed that East Asian power struggles have forever caught Korea in the crossfire, a major geo-political rub that is captured in the Korean proverb, "A shrimp's back is broken in a fight between whales". Largely for this reason, Korea now maintains an alliance with the United States, a policy described as "countering big neighbours by befriending distant powers". This course has maintained stability on the peninsula for over six decades and counting, and has allowed the region to blossom into one of the greatest economic engines in history. Today, Korea finds itself sandwiched between two of the world's largest markets, giving them hope that in an increasingly globalised economy, geography may finally have conferred upon Korea some singular advantages as a major commercial hub and gateway to East Asia.

Korea's undulating mountain paths recall the waves of a heavy sea, and put the densely-populated cities in perspective.

Measuring just less than 100,000 square kilometres, Korea is analogous in size to Hungary or the US state of Indiana, though it is so mountainous that it has often been said that if you flattened Korea with an iron, it would be bigger than China. To say that 70 per cent of Korea is mountainous gives you some idea of the terrain, but for visual effect I much prefer the description of early Christian missionaries to Korea, to whom the Korean landmass resembled "a sea in a heavy gale".

More than just a scenic backdrop, Korea's mountains are another geographical feature that has had many historical, cultural and social ramifications. Korea's jagged ridgelines have frequently blunted the full force of invasions by slowing the movements of armies and offering a multitude of natural redoubts to defenders. Coupled with Korea's size, the mountains also help ensure that cities are very dense, because unlike either Hungary (pop. 9.8 million) or Indiana (6.6 million), South Korea is home to 50 million people, nearly half of whom live in the capital region. Though this places a rather uncomfortable number of people in range of the North's big guns in the event of major hostilities, an old joke suggests that population density too may be a defence, as the North Korean tanks would be quickly bogged down in Seoul's rush-hour traffic.

HISTORY

The Korean people and their country are the ever-evolving product of thousands of years of human activity on the Korean peninsula, so no brief account of that story can hope to do more than trace the main threads that comprise the fabric of the Korea one encounters today.

Pre-history

Though archaeology tells us that hominids may have been living on the Korean peninsula for as long as half a million years, the people who came to be known as "The Koreans" claim an ancestry that reaches back over 4,000 years to a semi-mythical founder-king named Dangun. According to legends recorded by ancient Chinese and Korean scribes, a she-bear and a tigress who lived together in a cave prayed to the god Hwanung, and beseeched him to make them human. Hwanung gave them each a bunch of mugwort and 20 pieces of garlic, instructing them to eat it and avoid the sun for 100 days. The tigress soon gave up, but the bear did as she was instructed, and as a reward for her fortitude was transformed into a woman.

Sometime later, the woman was still without a husband, and so she again pleaded to Hwanung for intervention, which Hwanung personally obliged. The result of their union was a son, Wanggom, who founded the kingdom of Gojoseon in 2333 BC and became known as the king Dangun.

Though it would be a stretch to imagine that a homogeneous cultural line has flowed unbroken from Dangun to the present (let alone to suppose that he was actually the son of a god and a bear-woman), one can nonetheless glimpse in this foundational myth some of the telltale characteristics of the Koreans today: the perseverance in pursuit of a seemingly unattainable goal, the love of garlic, and an apparent soft spot for the poor-girl-rich-guy storyline, upon which innumerable seasons of modern K-dramas have been built. Some have even seen in this tale the earliest suggestion of a type of primitive kimchi, as a 100-day supply of garlic would seem to presuppose some method of fermentation or preservation.

The Three Kingdoms Period, (37 BC–668 AD)

Around the time of the birth of Christ, walled city-states arose around the peninsula, and during the first three centuries AD, these coalesced into federated states and finally into three powerful kingdoms: Baekche, which occupied the central and western parts of the peninsula, Shilla, which occupied the south and east, and Goguryeo, which covered the north and parts of what is today Manchuria. These were centralised states administered by an aristocracy, who acquired their status through hereditary succession.

It is during this period that Confucianism was introduced to the Korean peninsula from China; first in Goguryeo in 372, and then soon after in Baekche and Shilla. Confucian educational institutions were established and the Confucian classics were widely read and embraced by the ruling classes, who saw in Confucianism a way to maintain both the social order and their aristocratic status. Buddhism also arrived from China in the same year, and was likewise embraced by the aristocracy for its compatibility with the social order and its positive associations with the sophisticated and powerful Chinese.

The three kingdoms perpetually jockeyed with one another (and with the Chinese) for territory and power, and thus offer the modern observer an early glimpse of the intense regional rivalries that still complicate and confound Korean national politics. After many years of shifting borders and wrestling for control, it was Shilla who finally emerged dominant, unifying the peninsula under its rule in 668.

Unified Shilla Period (668-935)

Shilla unified the peninsula south of the 39th parallel and established their capital at Gyoungju, while remnants of the defeated Goguryeo withdrew north and created a state called Balhae in what are today the northern reaches of North Korea and southern Manchuria.

Shilla developed a sophisticated and outward-looking civilisation that liberally absorbed Chinese influences. Having yet no written language of their own, Koreans used a modified form of Chinese characters (called *idu*) to represent the Korean language, which encouraged a flowering of native philosophy, poetry and music. This period also marked Korea's first brush with intensive foreign language study, as monks and scholars mastered the original Confucian texts and produced works of their own entirely in Chinese.

A Buddhist monk beats a dharma drum, called *beopgo*, to signify the transference of Buddhist dharma to all sentient beings.

Cheomseongdae (stargazing platform) in Gyeongju dates to the seventh century and is believed to be the oldest surviving astronomical observatory in Asia.

Buddhism was firmly established as the state religion, and entered a Golden Age. A number of exquisite temples were built at this time, including a large temple in Gyoungju called Bulguksa, whose name itself ("Temple of the Land of Buddha") reflects the depth of their commitment to the imported creed. The capital is said to have had a population of one million people (which would have made it four times larger than its current population), and contemporary accounts describe it as a place of art, merrymaking, science and sophistication.

Balhae was not known for such heights of cultural achievement, but it was during their tenure that the *ondol* floor-heating system made its first appearance. By directing the fire from a furnace underneath a masonry floor and out through a chimney, the people of Balhae successfully warded off the harsh northern winters, and bequeathed to all subsequent generations of Koreans the simple luxury of basking on a toasty, heated floor, a pastime still common at saunas across the country.

In the middle of the 8th century, Shilla began to show signs of decline. Clan rivalries, mismanagement, and conflict between the monarchy, the aristocracy and religious leaders weakened the unity of the state, while military conflicts with the Chinese and Japanese undermined its strength. Commoners rebelled against the heavy taxes that were levied to fund the increasingly decadent lifestyle of the upper classes, while roving rebel bands gained in strength and acted with increasing impunity.

In the late 9th century, the breakaway states of Later Baekche and Later Goguryeo emerged, and this time it was Goguryeo, under the leadership of Wang Geon, who subdued the other two and emerged as the new unifier of the peninsula.

The Goryeo Dynasty (936-1392)

Wang Geon established a new kingdom which he called Goryeo ("high mountains and sparkling waters"), which is a shortening of Goguryeo and, in a slightly modified pronunciation, is the name by which "Korea" became known to the West.

Like Shilla before it, Goryeo was considered one of the most advanced civilisations of its time. Goryeo artisans created celadon pottery, which even contemporary Chinese widely considered to be the finest in the world; printers created the world's first movable metal type printing two centuries before Gutenberg; and Buddhist monks created the Tripitaka Koreana, a woodblock printing of the entire Buddhist canon that is still housed in Haeinsa Temple.

Also like Shilla, Goryeo liberally absorbed Chinese influence, and adopted many features of Chinese philosophy and statecraft. A civil service exam was instituted to select civil and military leaders (collectively called *yangban*), but in practice the exam was only open to members of aristocratic families, as farming families could neither afford the expense of preparing a son for the exam nor forgo his labour on the farm.

Unfortunately for Goryeo, their high-water mark coincided with the rise of the Mongols, upon whose to-do list the invasion of Goryeo was soon penciled in. From 1231 to 1259, a series of Mongol invasions devastated the Goryeo state, resulting in widespread destruction of life and property, the enslavement of thousands and major economic concessions that hobbled the Goryeo economy.

As a result, Goryeo became a vassal state of the Yuan Dynasty for the next 80 years. Mongol princesses were married off to Goryeo nobility and vice versa, effectively creating a marriage alliance. The Mongols treated the Korean peninsula much like a massive military base, breeding horses on Jeju Island and later conscripting Goryeo shipbuilders, sailors and soldiers in two doomed military adventures against the Japanese (which was not to be the last time that Koreans were pressed into service of the imperial ambitions of a larger nation).

When the Ming rose to challenge the Yuan in the late 14th century, the Goryeo court was split into pro-Yuan and pro-Ming factions. A general named Yi Seong-gye was dispatched to assist the Yuan, but instead turned his forces on the Goryeo leadership, overthrowing them and establishing the Joseon Dynasty, which would rule Korea through the dawn of the 20th century.

The Joseon Dynasty (1392-1910)

Yi established his capital in Seoul (then called Hanyang) and built walls around it, remnants of which are visible today. He called his new dynasty Joseon, recalling the original Kingdom of Gojoseon ("Old Joseon").

Yi and the new leadership were well aware of the deep loathing the commoners held for the elite, and the rancor among all levels of the upper classes, and strove to reorganise society to address these issues. Their solution was to adopt a state doctrine called Neo-Confucianism, a system of governmental and social reforms based on a strict reading of Confucian philosophy that would profoundly reshape Korean society and would institute many of the customs and traditions we recognise as "Korean" today.

Neo-Confucianists held that the father-son relationship was central to the functioning of a well-ordered state—"Never has there been a man who was filial at home who was not loyal to his king," went the teaching—and they thus held up filial piety as the chief virtue. From this period springs the tradition of venerating one's ancestors through the observance of rituals, a practice that has come down to our own time, though as we shall see, in somewhat modified form.

A Confucian scholar, or *seonbi*.

A top-to-bottom land reform was also carried out, which swept out the old order, rewarded Yi's loyalists, and greatly expanded the tax base of the new government. The *yangban* class was expanded, and the importance of the civil service exam greatly increased. Social classes were strictly separated, and intermarriage between *yangban* and commoners was prohibited.

The Neo-Confucianists condemned the extravagance of Buddhism and its concentrations of land and wealth, and blamed Buddhism for contributing to Goryeo's moral laxity and economic malaise. As a result, Buddhism was severely restricted and took refuge in the mountains, where it may still largely be found today, though it now enjoys the same freedoms as other faiths.

One of the biggest changes of the Joseon period concerned the rights and status of women. Unlike Goryeo women, who enjoyed relative freedom, women of the *yangban* classes in the Joseon Dynasty were obliged to follow the "Three Obediences": they had to obey their fathers when young, their husbands once married, and if widowed, their eldest son, who became the legal head of the household.

Twenty-seven kings would rule Joseon right down to the early 20th century, but it is the fourth Joseon king, Sejong the Great, who is the one most celebrated, and under whose wise and able leadership from 1418 to 1450 the Joseon Dynasty reached its apogee. Sejong encouraged and presided over several scientific and cultural achievements including the first rain gauge, a water clock, a revised calendar and an almanac to help farmers improve agricultural methods, but the one he is most remembered for today is the creation of the *Hangeul* alphabet by a group of scholars working under royal commission. Prior to the invention of *Hangeul*, the Korean language had been rendered in modified Chinese characters, which besides being difficult to learn, was less than ideally suited for representing the distinct sounds of Korean. Unlike Chinese, in which thousands of characters each represented individual words, *Hangeul* is a phonetic alphabet with a concise inventory of vowels and consonants that are relatively easy to learn.

This period also produced Korea's greatest military hero, Admiral Yi Sunshin. In 1592, the Korean peninsula was under assault by Japanese forces under Hideyoshi, who had landed over 150,000 crack troops in Busan with the ultimate aim of invading China. The Joseon land defenses were no match for the better-armed and combat-tested Japanese force, who swiftly ran riot over the peninsula, wreaking havoc and destruction wherever they went.

Joseon did however have a small but deadly naval force, featuring Admiral Yi's *Geobukseon* (Turtle Ships), which took their name from the spiked iron plating on their shell-like top which could both repel cannonballs and prevent men from boarding. Cannons bristled from the ship in all directions, including a dragon head on the prow which contained guns and

A replica of one of Admiral Yi's Turtle Ships housed at the War Memorial of Korea, Seoul.

poison smoke, which, because of the ships' manoeuvrability, could be deployed as a close-range chemical attack.

With these formidably armoured warships at his disposal, Yi cut off the Japanese supply lines, forcing them to retreat to Busan. When Hideyoshi gave it another go five years later, a mere dozen Turtle Ships under Yi's command annihilated an armada of three hundred Japanese warships off the coast of Mokpo, crippling Hideyoshi's war effort, which would finally end with his death in 1598. Joseon's experience with this and other foreign invasions led its leaders to pursue a policy of isolationism, earning Joseon the nickname "The Hermit Kingdom".

The Joseon Dynasty was relatively stable for hundreds of years, but in the 19th century it was in a state of terminal decline. Peasants who were suffering under exploitative conditions staged a series of popular revolts and uprisings. Joseon was also under heavy pressure from without, as powerful foreign nations pressed for the opening of the country and jockeyed with each for control of the peninsula. It was ultimately the Japanese, flush from their victories in the First Sino-Japanese War (1894-95) and the Russo-Japanese War (1904-05), who found themselves in a position to call the shots. In 1905, they forced King Gojong to sign a treaty with Japan that made Korea a protectorate and ceded much of their sovereignty to the Japanese; and in 1910, Japan formally annexed Korea as a colony. Though the loss of their national independence would turn out to be temporary, the Joseon Dynasty, which had ruled Korea for over 500 years, came to an end.

Japanese Colonial Period (1910-1945)

As a colony of Japan, Korea was administered by a Japanese Governor General and occupied by a large military presence. Korea's industrialisation, which had taken its first tentative steps in the late 19th century, was greatly accelerated, as large Japanese companies set up shop and the colonial government laid down roads, railroads and telegraph lines, though the lion's share of Korea's industrial and agricultural output was siphoned off to Japan. The colonisers also tried to efface Korean identity and absorb the Koreans culturally by restricting the use of the Korean language and forcing the Koreans to learn Japanese and adopt Japanese names. Today, one still finds many elderly Koreans who are able to speak Japanese.

During the Second World War, many Koreans were conscripted into Japan's war effort. Men were sent to work in mines and factories in Japan and Manchuria, while over 100,000 women and girls were pressed into sexual slavery as euphemistically-named "Comfort Women", which remains a major point of contention between the two countries today.

Many Koreans resisted the takeover, most famously on 1 March 1919, when independence activists in Seoul made a formal public declaration of independence from Japan, sparking rallies in the weeks that followed, which swelled to over a million people at hundreds of sites around the country. The police and military responded to the protests with brute force, killing and wounding thousands of protesters, and jailing and torturing many others. In the end, it was Japan's defeat in World War II in August 1945 that brought this painful chapter of Korean history to a close, though the legacy of this period continues to cast a long shadow over Korean-Japanese relations to the present day.

Division and War

With the bombing of Hiroshima on 6 August 1945, the end of the war was in sight, and US military leaders were worried that the fast-approaching Soviet army would quickly occupy the entire Korean peninsula. On 10 August, two US army colonels, acting without the benefit of time, preparation or even a sufficiently detailed map, drew a line dividing Korea along the 38th parallel to create two temporary zones for the Americans and the Soviets to administer while the Koreans established an independent national government. However, in 1948, this temporary division hardened into a de facto national border when ideological disagreements and Cold War machinations culminated in the election of separate governments: in the north, the Democratic People's Republic of Korea, headed by Kim Il-sung, and in the south, the Republic of Korea, led by Syngman Rhee.

Neither Kim nor Rhee saw the other as legitimate, and both desired a unified Korea, but it was Kim Il-sung who moved to unite them by force. On 25 June 1950, a large North Korean force equipped with 120 Soviet T-34 tanks surged across the 38th parallel and caught the relatively ill-equipped ROK and US defenders by surprise. Seoul was captured within days, and the US and ROK forces beat a hasty retreat south, eventually falling back into a defensive perimeter around the city of Busan.

US and UN troops were dispatched to Korea to shore up the Busan perimeter and build up forces for a breakout and counter-offensive. On 15 September, that moment arrived when General Douglas MacArthur made a daring amphibious attack at Incheon, which cut the thinly-stretched enemy supply lines and sent them fleeing back north. MacArthur gave chase deep into North Korea, pushing the routed

DPRK forces back toward the Chinese border and promising President Harry Truman that the war would be over by Christmas. The Chinese, fearful of having the US army so close to its border, spoiled MacArthur's Christmas plans by launching a massive counter-offensive that sent the US and UN forces reeling back again to well south of Seoul.

Under the capable leadership of General Matthew Ridgeway, the demoralised UN forces were whipped back into fighting shape, and rallied to recapture Seoul and push the battle line back into the north. For the next two years, the war settled into a bloody stalemate, ending in an armistice agreement on 27 July 1953. The agreement allowed for prisoner exchanges and created a buffer area called the Demilitarized Zone roughly where the original division had been drawn, but did not include a formal declaration of peace, which remains the case today and is why South and North Korea are still described as being "technically at war".

All told, nearly 40,000 UN troops were killed in the war (most of them American), and over 100,000 wounded. South Korean forces reported roughly 200,000 casualties, while the North Koreans and their Chinese allies lost a combined million men in uniform. The war was hardest of all on civilians. Though exact numbers are impossible to come by, an estimated 1.5 million were killed, while millions more were left wounded, destitute and homeless.

KOREA'S POST-WAR DEVELOPMENT

Korea's precarious situation in the 1940s and 1950s made their political, economic and social development—indeed their very survival as a nation—seem very unlikely. The "Miracle on the Han River" was a term coined to capture their breathtaking rise from the ashes to become a major economic power, but no less impressive was what might be called Korea's Second Miracle: the transition from a country ruled by military and civilian dictatorships into one of the most stable and robust democracies in Asia.

"The Miracle on the Han"

When the fighting subsided in 1953, few would have predicted a rosy future for South Korea. Cities and towns lay in utter ruin, particularly Seoul, which had been captured and re-taken four times in all and, according to many contemporary observers, was left with nary a brick standing atop another. The South Korean economy, not very highly developed to begin with, was a shambles, while the increasingly authoritarian and incompetent administration of Syngman Rhee proved incapable of getting the country on its feet.

In 1960, popular protests forced Rhee to step down, and after a brief and turbulent attempt at democracy, an army general named Park Chung-hee seized power in a May 1961 coup. Believing that putting Korea on a stable economic footing was a higher priority than democratic government, Park seized the reins and set the country on a path toward export-led development. Toward this end, he cultivated the rise of large conglomerates, called *chaebol*, which, in exchange for cheap government loans, market protection and monopoly status, were expected to conform to state-directed national development plans. To fund his ambitious designs in the face of dwindling foreign aid, Park secured cash from several sources: a controversial reparations agreement with Japan netted Korea several hundreds of millions of dollars; a further billion dollars was earned by supplying soldiers and contractors to the US war effort in Vietnam; and the remittances of overseas workers in Germany provided another source of much-needed capital.

Lacking natural resources, Park drew on the Korean people themselves, a vast source of labour that was cheap, well educated and highly responsive to nationalistic appeals for patience, diligence and sacrifice. This potent combination fuelled a dramatic rise in Korea's GDP and per capita income from the mid-1960s onward, and provided the corporate and industrial foundation for Korea's economic metamorphosis from a country that exported plywood, wigs and cement, into one whose cars, smartphones and flat-screen televisions would come to dominate markets around the world. In their race to close the gap with the major economic powers, Korean firms adopted a "fast follower" strategy, reverse-engineering imported technologies and producing domestic versions that were competitively priced and equal (in some cases, superior) to the originals in quality and service, and this development model worked well for a long time.

In 1997, the mostly uninterrupted rise of the Korean economy suffered a major setback, when the collapse of the Thai baht in July sent shockwaves through many other Asian economies. Several Korean *chaebol* who had borrowed heavily to fund their ambitious expansion plans suddenly found themselves to be insolvent, banks tottered under the weight of a mass of non-performing loans, the stock prices of Korean firms nose-dived and the value of the Korean won against the US dollar virtually halved overnight. The International Monetary Fund provided a bailout package to Korea, attached to strict remedies that saw many banks close, many companies of all sizes declare bankruptcy and thousands of workers made redundant.

Korea responded to the so-called "IMF crisis" in much the same way it responded to the crisis of post-war reconstruction in general: by rolling up their sleeves and digging themselves out. By 2001, the nearly 60-billion-dollar loan was paid off three years ahead of schedule, and Korea Incorporated was back on track.

Shared Sacrifice

During the IMF Crisis, many South Koreans responded to calls to share the burden of paying off the IMF loan. One of the most striking examples of shared sacrifice was when millions of people donated gold—in the form of wedding rings, trophies, medals, and jewellery—to help pay down the national debt. Though the sum collected amounted to a small percentage of what was owed, it was a dramatic illustration of the willingness of the South Korean people to band together in times of crisis, in a way that was hard for me to imagine happening anywhere else.

Korea's Second Miracle: Democracy

Despite having taken power by force, Park Chung-hee handily won re-election in 1967 on the strength of his undeniable economic achievements, but his increasing authoritarianism had begun to rankle the public, who began resisting his attempts to indefinitely prolong his rule. A particular object of public ire was the Yushin Constitution, enacted in 1972, which placed strict limits on civil society while tightening Park's grip on the reigns of state. Popular discontent escalated throughout the 1970s as protests rocked university campuses across the country, while internal discord over the best way forward split Park's inner circle. The situation came to a head on the evening of 26 October 1979, when Kim Jae-gyu, a longtime Park confidant and head of the Korean Central Intelligence Agency, shot Park and his bodyguard to death as the three of them were eating dinner.

Park's death did not however result in the desired democratic reforms, as another general named Chun Doo-hwan seized control of the government within weeks of the assassination. Chun's refusal to discard the deeply unpopular Yushin Constitution and his heavy-handed tactics generated opposition that was swift and intense. Protests again sprang up in several cities, most notably in Gwangju, where in May of 1980 citizens staged an uprising and managed to secure control of the city after days of roving street battles in which soldiers fired indiscriminately into crowds of civilians. A few days later, Chun sent tanks and elite military units into the city and put a bloody end to what is now commonly referred to as the "Gwangju Uprising".

Civilian casualty figures are disputed and range from 144 (which is the figure given by the Martial Law Command) to well over a thousand, with hundreds more wounded and several dozen missing and presumed dead. Chun's pyrrhic victory in Gwangju would come back to haunt him: in 1996 he was sentenced to death for his role in the massacre (though he was later pardoned), but more immediately, his actions that week effectively torpedoed whatever chance he might have had at establishing legitimacy and dogged him for the rest of his deeply unpopular administration.

Toward the end of his term, Chun began manoeuvring to anoint another military man, Roh Tae-woo, as his successor, which finally pushed public discontent to critical mass. In the summer of 1987, the largest protests to date (popularly known as "The June Uprising") were joined by hundreds of thousands of people from all walks of life who united in opposition to continued military dictatorship. Faced with the distasteful prospect of violently suppressing a massive popular protest one year before Seoul was to host the Summer Olympics, Chun ceded to the public's demands for presidential elections, the release of political prisoners and the restoration of political rights to the popular dissident, Kim Dae-jung.

Fair and open elections were held later that year, but the results were disappointing to pro-democracy activists: two opposition candidates, Kim Dae-jung and Kim Young-sam, decided to run separately, thus splitting the opposition vote and handing victory to Roh. The subsequent election of Kim Young-sam in 1992 thus marked the first time in Korean history that the office of president was peacefully transferred to a member of an opposition party.

Since 1992, Koreans have gone to the polls four more times to select their president, with each election further solidifying the tradition of democratic governance. Though ideological divides can be wide and the day-to-day workings of the National Assembly can be rancorous, Korea today is one of the most stable democracies in Asia, an outcome that was hard to imagine just thirty years ago.

CONTEMPORARY KOREA

For much of its history, South Korea has been an avid absorber of influences from other countries, an openness that is still evident today in a range of cultural milieu, from food to football to philosophy. Since the 1990s, a loose collaboration between government and industry has been working to extend Korea's soft-power influence and boost cultural exports to Asia and beyond, a general trend which is encompassed in the term *Hallyu* ("Korean Wave"). By promoting Korean cultural products (film, food, TV dramas, music) around the world, *Hallyu* has contributed greatly in rebranding South Korea from an impoverished cultural backwater to the hip, high-tech home of slick pop stars and cutting-edge film auteurs, and as a prime mover in beauty, fashion and technology trends.

In 1996, South Korea placed another feather in its economic cap when it was invited to join the Organization for Economic Cooperation and Development (OECD), through which Koreans have since been sharing their development expertise with other nations. In 1991, Korea established the Korea International Cooperation Agency (KOICA), a development assistance program similar to the American Peace Corps (who were active in South Korea from 1966 to 1981), that has sent thousands of volunteers to countries around the world, and has contributed to earning South Korea the distinction of being the only country to transform itself from a net receiver of aid to a net donor in the span of a generation.

Today, the Korean economy again finds itself at a crossroads. Rising, low-cost manufacturers in China and elsewhere have eroded Korea's ability to compete on price, and are lending a life-or-death urgency for Korea to move upmarket, innovate and evolve. The militaristic *chaebol-*

led development model worked well for a country playing catch-up to other industrial players, but far less well for a country that desires to incubate and lead the industries of the future. To do so will require sea changes in the increasingly anachronistic *chaebol*-dominated business landscape, as well as an equally profound re-ordering of educational priorities, corporate structure and cultural sensibilities. Many of these changes are already well underway and, if successful, promise to radically transform Korea in ways that must seem every bit as improbable to young Koreans today as the promise of today's Korea once seemed to their parents and grandparents. Time will tell whether Korea can successfully retool for the challenges of the 21st century global economy, but in light of their recent history, it seems wise not to bet against it.

CHAPTER 3

VALUES

> ❝The all-round Korean will be a Confucian in society, a Buddhist when he philosophizes, and a spirit worshipper when he is in trouble.❞

> **— Homer B Hulbert,**
> **19th-century Christian missionary**

RELIGION IN KOREA

South Korea is a religiously plural and tolerant society with no true majority religion. Slightly over half of Koreans are affiliated with either Buddhism (23%) or Christianity (29%), and just under half claim no religious affiliation. The ethical-philosophical system of Confucianism has also long provided another deep and intertwined layer to the social, cultural and political mix. And running through, under and alongside these belief systems are ancient folk beliefs like shamanism which have animated the Korean spirit since pre-historic times and still find various forms of popular expression. Throughout history, these various traditions have co-existed in varying degrees of harmony and tension, but none can be said to lay exclusive claim on Korean hearts and minds. The general Korean openness to religion was well captured by the 19th century Christian missionary Homer B Hulbert, who wrote that, "The all-round Korean will be a Confucian in society, a Buddhist when he philosophizes, and a spirit worshipper when he is in trouble."

CONFUCIANISM

Of all the major philosophical traditions that have taken root in Korea, none have had a more transformative impact than Confucianism, which was first introduced to Korea in the

4th century AD. Confucianism got its start with the Chinese philosopher Kong Fuzi (552–479 BC), and has undergone many modifications and permutations over the centuries. Opinions differ over whether it is to be called a religion, as Confucianism generally concerns itself not with the afterlife but with the affairs of this world and the principles for creating a just and harmonious society. Toward that end, Confucian philosophy delineates five cardinal relationships (more on those later) and codifies their associated virtues and mutual responsibilities, which have been expressed over the centuries through ritual and etiquette that permeated all aspects of civil and social life and are still evident today, though in more subtle or attenuated forms.

Contemporary Korea is no longer strictly ordered by Confucian principles, nor is Confucianism the official state doctrine as it was during the Joseon Dynasty. However, its long insinuation into all levels of society, which shaped attitudes and guided human interactions right down to the way verbs are conjugated, doesn't merely dissipate with the appearance of a democratic, industrialised society. Though the average Korean today doesn't walk around identifying himself as a Confucianist any more than the average North American or European thinks of himself as an Aristotelian nor grounds his daily decisions by consciously referring to ancient Greek philosophy, those undercurrents are nonetheless perceptible in many of the modern Korean's habits, dispositions and institutions, whether he consciously appeals to them or not.

So great was the influence of Confucianism on Korea that it's impossible to even begin talking about Korean culture without it, but a few caveats are in order. To say that Korea is "Confucian" is to make a statement about an underlying current of history that informs modern life; it is not the all-pervasive and irresistible force that some imagine it to be. Upon learning about Korea's Confucian tradition, a common temptation for many observers is to over-apply Confucianism as a means of explaining everything from plane crashes to the way people navigate a shopping cart through the grocery store, even sometimes using it to justify seemingly contradictory positions. Like all ideologies that aim to reshape society, from Christianity to communism, Confucianism was never perfectly applied, and has long been merely one factor—albeit a powerful one—in the mix of impulses, ideas, dispositions and imperatives that have competed for and shaped the Korean soul throughout the ages.

Another thing to bear in mind is that the Korea of today is a society undergoing a profound and fraught process of re-examining, revising and occasionally discarding many of its old values in light of the demands of a highly-mobile democratic society. Confucian respect for the ruling class strikes many modern Koreans as quaint, as corruption scandals dog successive political leaders and engender public cynicism. In business, the old hierarchies have likewise shown signs of cracking, as reformers try to make room for young innovators, who have long been stifled by little more than their age. Loyalty to the company, once an unshakeable commandment, is under strain as well, as many firms are sometimes obliged to lay off workers, while workers express an increased willingness to jump ship to further their own careers if the opportunity arises. Wives who would have been obliged to stay home years ago now work, as more empowered and highly-educated women plant their stakes in the workplace. And what should one conclude about Korea's fealty to the Confucian reverence for age in a society with rising rates of poverty among the elderly and a growing number of "silver towns" (assisted living facilities) superseding the old injunction to care for one's elders and live with them under one roof? In short, to view Korea through a strictly Confucian lens is to overlook the many ways that Korea is changing.

In the 2002 FIFA World Cup, the South Korean national team, coached by Dutch-born manager Guus Hiddink, went on a historic run to the semi-finals, despite never having won a single game in five previous World Cup appearances. Hiddink's methods were subsequently dissected and analysed in a blizzard of books, editorials and water-cooler conversations, and the consensus was that along with his heightened emphasis on fitness and some tactical reordering, a major key to success lay in minimising the influence of Confucianism on and off the pitch. Older players or those with family connections were no longer guaranteed a place on the team; players in their early 20s were given a chance to earn starting spots, get their touches, and shine; while all were obliged to eat, work out and live together in training, in order to break down hierarchies and create an atmosphere of equality and solidarity. Hiddink's unprecedented success gave Koreans a sweet and striking taste of the power of blending a strong work ethic with meritocracy, and gave reform-minded young leaders a jolt that reverberates today.

Education

Koreans' legendary commitment to education is another attitude with clear roots in the Confucian tradition. Confucius taught that all people were alike in their basic nature, and it was only in their habits that they differed. Education thus was elevated to great importance, as it was the way to produce good habits and virtuous people. During the Joseon Dynasty, a civil service exam was for a long time the only way to get ahead and gain status in society, and required years of arduous study of the classic Confucian texts. As far back as the Shilla Dynasty, Korean scholars went to China to master and translate these texts, and great Confucian scholars (two of whom, Yi I and Yi Hwang, appear on Korean banknotes today) were revered.

While the contributions of Confucian ideology are often noted, Korea's educational achievements also owe a debt to the country's other religious and philosophical traditions. An obvious role for education is for example apparent in the Buddhist teaching that nirvana can be achieved through continual self-improvement, and Buddhist temples have long served as repositories of wisdom and learning. Protestant missionaries established many libraries, schools and universities, some of which (like Yonsei and Ehwa) have grown to become the top universities in the country.

Education again became key in the second half of the 20th century, when a rapidly industrialising economy created a pressing need for a highly skilled and educated workforce. It is sometimes said that an "education miracle" preceded the economic miracle, as President Park Chung-hee's ambitious development plans were able to tap into a populace whose education levels gave them a leg up on countries like Chile and Mexico who had GDPs several times greater than South

Korea's at the time.

As university enrolment accelerated in the 1970s and 1980s, it became important to distinguish oneself by getting into a top university, spurring a cycle of competition that today is more appropriately described as a craze. Today, getting the best education one can afford is considered more important than ever, as greater competition for jobs has greatly intensified the competition to gain a coveted spot in one of the so-called "SKY" universities (Seoul National University, Koryo University and Yonsei University), or a top-flight university overseas. The race starts as early as pre-school, and intensifies as the years go by, peaking in the non-stop grind of high school, when students clock 18-hour days to prepare for the dreaded *suneung* (university entrance exam), the high-stakes test that has an outsized bearing on their career trajectory and prospects. On the day of the *suneung* exam, every third-year high school student (called "*go-sam*") in Korea flocks to a test centre, sometimes receiving police escort if they are running late, while thousands of mothers stand vigil at the gates, clutching prayer beads and praying for their young scholar's success.

The intense educational environment is not without its social, emotional and economic costs. The pressure to succeed and the gloomy prospect of failure contribute to Korea's high rates of suicide, which are the highest in the OECD for several years running and is the leading cause of death of Koreans aged 10 to 39. Despite government efforts to keep private education costs under control, many Korean parents spend up to a third of their income on *hagwons* (private academies) to help their son or daughter bone up on tough subjects, get a leg up on their peers, or merely to keep up with a school curriculum that covers a lot of ground in a short time. Many families with the means send a child (often accompanied by mom) to attend school for a year or two in an English-speaking country, while the *gireogi appa* ("goose father")—so-called because he must travel a long distance to see his family—remains behind in Korea to work.

The importance of education in Korea, however, runs deeper than merely getting ahead. "Isn't it a pleasure to study, and to practice what you have learned?" said Confucius, who taught that to be well educated was to be fully human. For many, this love of learning doesn't survive the pressure cooker of preparing for the university entrance exam, but one does meet many other Koreans today for whom education did not stop with the completion of their formal schooling.

As a teacher, I have met many Koreans, young and old, who find intrinsic value in studying and see it as a lifelong pursuit, and have witnessed them taking classes in community centres, universities, city halls and public libraries in a variety of subjects, simply because they enjoy it. My wife, a harried business owner and full-time mother of three, is fairly typical: she studies English online daily (and constantly peppers me with new slang I've never heard), regularly attends seminars to stay on top of her field and is currently taking a class in candle-making.

In Korea, knowledge isn't just power, it's actually cool, and there's no stigma attached to being a nerd. Achievements in a laboratory are often as admired as skill on a football pitch, and bespectacled scientists, programmers and software developers occasionally attain star status. Just as the Confucian scholar was celebrated in ages past, the most popular kid in school today (and the envy of every mother) is not the star athlete or the prom queen but the valedictorian.

Hierarchy

Another of the lasting influences of Confucianism was the elaboration of social hierarchies in Korea. Confucianism described a well-ordered society in terms of five cardinal relationships, and the principal virtues that were to characterise them:

Between king and subject there is justice.
Between father and son there is closeness.
Between husband and wife there is separation of duties.
Between senior and junior there is order.
Between friend and friend there is trust.

Except for the friend relationship, all others were vertical, and required deference from the subordinate party while requiring the superior to act with justice, wisdom and benevolence or risk undermining his authority.

This sense of one's place in the social order is still pervasive in Korean society today and is reflected in every sentence a Korean utters. Verbs are conjugated according to status, with *banmal* (informal speech) used with peers or people beneath your station, while speaking to those above you requires the use of polite speech forms (called *jondaetmal*). Korean companies are very hierarchical, and can have a bewildering array of titles, but each person in the organisation knows exactly where he stands, what he can expect from his staff and what he needs to do for the boss. Subordinates owe loyalty and deference to those above, while those higher up the ladder are expected to treat their juniors with fairness and benevolence.

In such a system, knowing the relative ages of the people you meet is important, which is the reason that the question that most often follows "Where are you from?" is "How old are you?" Older friends, relatives and associates are called by one of many honorific titles (See Chapter 8: Learning the Language), never by name. Even among twins, the one who came second must forever use these forms to address the ever-so-slightly older one.

Even in the often anonymous world of the Internet, Korean attention to status sometimes ripples through in interesting ways. Back in 2001, I used to play an online PC game called *Diablo II*, and I noticed that Korean players were using the honorific title *hyoungnim* in the in-game text chat to address players who lived in different cities and whom they had never interacted with nor met in real life. How did they determine who was to be called *hyoungnim*? By whoever had the higher level character.

Like all things, the deference shown to elders has changed with the times, but also shows a remarkable stability. While you're less likely to see people springing from their seats on the bus to offer it to the elderly lady or gentleman who has just boarded, it does happen and is still considered good form (though just to be safe, many cities have now reserved seating for elderly passengers). One still must wait for the oldest member of the party to eat before you may begin eating, to listen attentively when he or she speaks and to avoid openly disagreeing with or contradicting them. I've also even seen elderly passers-by scold young children in the street, and though some kids are inclined to blow it off, I am continually amazed that many not only listen but take it to heart.

In many Western countries, respect is often thought of as something earned, not merely granted as a reward for sticking around longer than everyone else. Perhaps for this reason, many Western expats report that one of the hardest aspects of Korean culture to get used to is the practice of showing automatic respect for age. There are times when the Korean system works beautifully: grandmothers get seats on the bus, and elderly gentlemen get a full hearing. But it becomes much harder to swallow (for Koreans too) when we are obliged to defer to the occasional person who, whether due to incompetence, stupidity or a disagreeable character, would garner little or no respect otherwise. Though it's much easier said than done, the best course in such cases is to restrain your cultural instincts, offer whatever respect is due and take a small measure of solace in the thought that if you ever become an old curmudgeon yourself, there will be at least one country in the world that will still make you feel special sometimes.

Family

Confucian thought placed special emphasis on the family. Of all the Confucian virtues, the most important is filial piety, as it was seen as the lynchpin of society from the family up to the state level, or as Confucius more elegantly put it, "Never has there been a man who was filial at home who was not loyal to his king." Children from a young age are taught to obey and respect their parents and older relatives, while the elders are imbued with a strong sense of duty and responsibility to care for their dependents and raise them to be good people. The imperative to demonstrate filial piety extends even long after a family member's death, and is embodied in the *jesa* ceremony, ancestor memorial rites that are performed on major holidays and on the anniversary of a parent's or grandparent's passing to honour them and express one's unending gratitude.

In the past decade or so, social, economic and cultural pressures have been pushing family dynamics in new directions. In past generations, Koreans were far more likely to live with three or four generations under one roof, with the eldest son taking on the responsibility of caring for his elderly parents. Much has changed in this regard, as a rapidly aging society places burdens on a smaller pool of younger people, many of whom opt to place their elderly parents in assisted living facilities called "silver towns". Today, Koreans are more likely to live with their nuclear families than with extended family networks, and a large and increasing number of young Koreans are opting to move into their own places prior to getting married, something that was virtually unheard of a decade or two ago.

Elderly people are today more likely to live alone than they were in the past.

Gender Roles

Traditional Confucian gender roles have also left their imprint on modern Korean society. In the Joseon Dynasty, the woman's primary role was childrearing and maintaining the home, and they were referred to as *ansaram* ("inside person") to reflect what was then thought to be their proper domain in a Confucian society. In their familial relationships, they were to submit to the "Three Obediences": to their fathers when young, to their husbands when they married and if they were widowed, to their eldest son, who became the legal head of household. Women had no rights of inheritance, no access to education and were obliged to cover their faces on the rare occasions they ventured from the house.

Modern Korean women have made great strides in some areas, but still lag in others. Secondary education is now widespread, and increasing numbers of women have joined the workforce. In 2012, South Korea even elected its first female president, Park Geun-hye. Though she certainly benefitted from her family pedigree as the daughter of former president Park Chung-hee, her election was nonetheless a significant event in a country where women were once barred from having any role in public affairs whatsoever.

The Korean government has been slowly dismantling some of the legal obstacles to female empowerment, but many long-standing social and cultural barriers remain. South Korea has the highest gender pay gap of any OECD country for several years running, and has made little progress in closing it. Despite the passage of laws designed to combat unfair hiring practices, women still report unfair treatment in job interviews, in which they are asked about their marriage plans, their weight, their plans to have children and other questions that have no bearing on their qualifications. Though Korean society appears to be moving in the right direction on reducing gender inequality, progress is slow and there remains a long way to go.

BUDDHISM

Buddhism was introduced to Korea in the early Three Kingdoms period (late 4th century) from China, and was soon adopted by the kings of all three: first in Goguryeo in 372, then Baekche in 384, and finally Shilla in 572. Initially, Buddhism was the religion of the ruling class, who associated it positively with the advanced civilisation of China and saw it as a way to strengthen royal authority. Over time, it trickled down to the common people, who found it to be compatible with pre-existing folk traditions and blended the two in many ways.

The Shilla period saw a flowering of Buddhist art and architecture, including magnificent, sprawling temples like Bulguksa and the Seokkuram Grotto, where a large granite Buddha has been placidly witnessing every sunrise since its completion in 774, and which in 1995 was designated a UNESCO World Heritage site. Because of national treasures like these, the old Shilla capital of Gyoungju is today a major tourist draw and remains the best place to get a sense of why the Shilla Dynasty is referred to as the Golden Age of Korean Buddhism.

In the Goryeo Period as well, Buddhism enjoyed great cultural, social and political influence. Monks were allowed to sit for civil service examinations and earn official titles, Buddhist landholdings were exempted from taxation and monks acted as advisors to the kings. It was during this period that monks created the Tripitaka Koreana—over 80,000 hand-carved, wooden printing blocks in Hanja characters that records the most comprehensive collection of Buddhist scripture in the Chinese language.

During the Joseon period, Neo-Confucianist scholars blamed Goryeo's decline on Buddhism, and thus greatly restricted its practice. Many Buddhist temples and landholdings were lost, and Buddhist monks were barred from urban centres. In response, Buddhism retreated to the countryside, where it still remained popular with common people and is largely to be found today. Despite their reduced status, Buddhists still contributed to the country in important ways, most famously during the Hideyoshi invasions of the late 16th century, when groups of warrior-monks won several key battles against the invaders.

A Buddhist monk in traditional attire.

Because of this long suppression, the dawn of the 20th century found Buddhism at a low ebb, but it started to make a slow comeback during the Japanese colonial period. The number of professed adherents continued to rise throughout the 20th century, though by then it was competing with Christianity, which had recently arrived and enjoyed the advantage of being based in growing urban centres.

Today, approximately 22 million Koreans claim Buddhist affiliation, and they can be seen worshipping at the country's many temples, and grey-robed monks are again a common sight in cities around the country. South Korea also celebrates Buddha's birthday as a national holiday. On this day, temples large and small are decorated with colourful lanterns, to which the faithful attach their prayers for health, prosperity, their child's admission to Harvard and other blessings.

Tripitaka Koreana

Because of its close association with the state, Buddhism has always had a national character and was long thought to protect the nation in times of war, a belief which has earned Korean Buddhism the moniker *hoguk*, or, "protect the nation" Buddhism. It was this belief that spurred Goryeo monks to action in the 11th century, when recurring threats of Khitan invasion inspired them to carve a complete set of Buddhist scriptures in order to please the Buddha and secure his protection. The original set survived the Khitans but was destroyed two centuries later by the Mongols. The Goryeo court thus had it carved again, this time totalling over 81,000 pages, each recorded on a separate block, which is said to be without any known errors and to have taken sixteen years and Buddha-only-knows how many monks to complete. This version survived the Mongols and all subsequent invasions, and is housed in Haein Temple near the city of Daegu. The Tripitaka Koreana was designated a UNESCO World Heritage Site in 1995, so it seems safe to say—knock on wood—that the Buddha would be pleased.

CHRISTIANITY

Christianity first arrived in Korea in 1784, when a Confucian scholar named Yi Seong-hun, who had recently been baptised a Roman Catholic in Beijing, returned to Korea and began converting other scholars to his new faith. The small community of Catholics very soon ran afoul of Confucian authorities for refusing to perform ancestor memorial rites, which Confucian leaders regarded as an important ritual expression of social stability and a cultural pillar of state authority. In 1791, the fledgling Korean Church had its first martyr when Paul Yun (formerly Yun Ji-chung) was beheaded for failing to perform the Confucian memorial service for his deceased mother. Many thousands more Catholics were put to death in the century that followed, 93 of whom would be canonised—along with ten French priests who came to Korea to propagate the faith—by Pope John Paul II in 1984, giving Korea the most saints of any country outside of Europe.

In 1884, the first Protestants began arriving, and found a weakening Joseon court that was more tolerant of their ministry. Early Protestant missionaries built hospitals, schools and universities (some of which became the best universities in the country), and were thus seen by the Joseon court as a modernising force as much as a religious one. Their message of equality in God's eyes also resonated deeply with a population that was fed up with being subservient to a bloated aristocracy, and the new faith's close association with an increasingly prosperous United States fired their dreams of a better life in the here-and-now.

During the Japanese colonial period, many prominent Protestants resisted Japanese rule, and soon acquired a reputation as devout nationalists, further burnishing Christianity's positive image. In the late 20th century, as rapid industrialisation impelled many workers to flock to urban centres, the churches served as focal points of new communities for people who had been uprooted from small villages around the country.

Today, roughly one in five Koreans are Protestant, a remarkable percentage considering that there were none at all a little over a century ago. Churches dot the cityscapes, some of which claim massive congregations. The Yoido Full Gospel Church in Seoul numbers its flock at roughly half a million, and is said to have the largest congregation in the world.

SHAMANISM

The first religion to appear on the Korean peninsula was shamanism, a form of animistic belief that is thought to have originated in central Asia, and dates back tens of thousands of years, long before Dangun was a sparkle in Mother Bear's eye. Though shamanism has no unified body of belief or dogma, no central authority or church and few or no shrines or structures devoted to it, it has nonetheless both influenced and incorporated influences from other religions over the centuries.

At its core, animist belief holds that the natural world is populated by a myriad of spirits; inanimate objects are thought to have a form of consciousness, and the souls of deceased humans are believed to roam the earth, capable of causing mischief in the affairs of the living. A shaman, usually a woman known as a *mudang*, is thought to have the ability to act as a medium through which the world of the living and the spirit realm may communicate. At a young age, the future *mudang* receives a calling in the form of a mental disturbance known as *sinbyeong* ("spiritual sickness"), after which an experienced *mudang* will take her on as an apprentice until she is ready to strike out on her own.

One of the main functions of the *mudang* is to perform a ritual called *gut*, which is usually commissioned to remedy a problem like a serious illness, a run of misfortune or to placate the restless spirit of someone who has died prematurely. The *gut* can be small and involve only the *mudang* and client, or it can be quite large and involve several *mudang* and musicians and cost several millions of won (thousands of US dollars). During a *gut*, the *mudang* wear colourful outfits which they change for different phases of the ceremony, and they may perform feats like walking on the edge of a knife blade to demonstrate power and courage to the spirits. The precise features of the ceremony can vary according to purpose, region and personal style, but in general the *mudang* may sing, howl, laugh, dance, chant and otherwise beckon the spirit she wishes to contact. Once contact is made, she acts as a medium through which attendees can beseech the spirit, and the spirit can communicate its wishes or grievances to the living.

Mudang are also often employed as sympathetic counsellors to people struggling with personal problems or pressing questions—an important function in a society which still attaches a stigma to psychological counselling and psychotherapy—and are sometimes called upon to bless the opening of a new business or christen a ship.

Despite many official attempts to suppress it, shamanist beliefs and practices have shown a remarkable resilience and adaptability throughout history. Because it is flexible, non-dogmatic and places few demands on practitioners, many Koreans, including many Buddhists and Christians, partake of it in some form or another without necessarily identifying themselves as "shamanist" or finding irreconcilable conflict with their professed faith.

JUYEOK

Though a *mudang* can sometimes be consulted as a sort of seer or advisor, there is another branch of fortune telling, called *juyeok*, which derives from the ancient Chinese philosophy embodied in the *I Ching* (The Book of Changes). Unlike the *mudang*, who consults the spirit world for guidance, the *yeoksulga* (fortune teller) determines the best course of action by considering the person's *saju* ("four pillars"), which collectively refers to the year, month, day and time of birth. Other tools of divination may include a set of special sticks or colourful *hwatu* playing cards, or may involve counting the brush strokes in a person's name. Traditionally, most fortune tellers were blind, as this was one of the only means of work available to them, while their handicap was also thought by many to give them ability to better see the future.

Though it still has a core of adherents, fortune telling is treated with skepticism by most Koreans today and with derision by many others, many of whom nonetheless admit to doing it for fun or out of curiosity. In any city in Korea, one may find many *cheolhakgwan* (literally "philosophy institute"), which is often as simple as a small tent on a city street, where people may stop to ask a fortune teller a question: whether a couple is compatible, the appropriate day to schedule a C-section, the university one's son or daughter should apply to, an important business decision or some such question of particular concern.

Despite widespread skepticism, fortune tellers tents like the one pictured here are still a common sight in Korean cities.

Fortune tellers are still very often consulted in order to select an auspicious name for an expectant mother's child, or in some cases, to suggest a new name for an adult whose current name is judged to be misaligned with his *saju* and is thus suspected to be the cause of persistent misfortune. Some professional baseball players have legally changed their names on the advice of a fortune teller after a protracted hitting slump, as in the case of the Lotte Giants outfielder Son A-seop (formerly Son Gwang-min), who at this writing boasts an impressive .323 career batting average and has a starting job sewn up.

STEREOTYPES AND REALITY

Because Korea is a predominantly mono-ethnic society, it may be tempting to think that there is a uniformity of values, feelings, opinions and practices, and that Koreans generally want the same things and go about getting them the same way. The most cursory observation of the debates on the floor of Korea's National Assembly or of the discussion board of any Korean website will quickly disabuse anyone of the notion that Koreans are inclined to think alike and seek harmony in all things, and the same diversity is evident throughout the society: the whole range of human striving, ability, emotion, temperament and sensibility is on display in Korea all the time if we merely tune in to it.

What we end up perceiving is partly a function of our own outlook, a human propensity that is captured well in the old parable about the traveller on his way to an unfamiliar town. As he draws up to the outskirts, he stops and asks a farmer what kind of people he can expect to find there, to which the farmer replies with a question, "What were the people like in the place you left?"

"Mostly a bunch of dishonest, lazy, rude people," says the man, "I couldn't wait to get out of there!"

Sorry," says the farmer, "but I think you're going to find the people up here to be the same."

Sometime later, a second traveller who is heading to the same town stops and asks the farmer the same question, and the farmer asks him, "What were the people like in the place you left?"

"They were mostly honest, hardworking, considerate folks. I was really sorry to leave!"

"Cheer up!" says the farmer, "You're going to find the same kind of people around here."

Having said that, any group of people that speaks a common language and inhabits the same corner of the earth for so long is bound to share some broad similarities and cultural touchstones. Though none of the many facets of culture are completely impervious to the demands of modernity, global capitalism, technological progress and demographic shifts, many time-honoured practices and beliefs still manage to find expression and allow us to speak of a thing called "Korean culture".

THE GROUP VS THE INDIVIDUAL

In contrast to many Western countries' emphasis on the individual, Korean society has a more "collectivist" orientation; not in the sense of 1950s Soviet farming, but in an observable tendency to create and maintain long term commitments to various groups and to observe established norms vis-a-vis other in-group members. Because of this group orientation, Koreans assign a high value to loyalty, and display a greater willingness to suspend their own wishes in the interest of group solidarity, harmony and long-term mutual benefit. The consequences of disregarding one's social obligations or being cut off from the group can be particularly harsh. The willing loner is a rare bird; to be a *wangtta* (outcast) sadly results in bullying, depression, and too often, suicide.

This tendency to band together can be seen in Korea's agricultural past, when farmers relied on community networks and mutual assistance to harvest crops more efficiently. The cartoonist Wonbok Rhie also traces this impulse to times of invasion, when the royal court sometimes fled the capital, leaving the common people to fend largely for themselves—which also may shed some light on their feelings about political leaders more generally. Add to this historical backdrop the Confucian emphasis on loyalty to one's in-group, and you have a few key ingredients for a powerful social adhesive that still binds Korean people to each other in a variety of ways.

Social networking is a universal human tendency, but it perhaps approaches its peak expression in Korea, where the average person maintains (or tries very hard to maintain) affiliations with various official and unofficial groups, teams, professional associations, social clubs, alumni organisations

The bonds Koreans form in their school years often last a lifetime.

and the like. The tendency to network can begin even in infancy, as Korean mothers try to get their newborn into the best *sanhu joriwon* (post-natal care facility) they can afford, in the hope of making beneficial and lasting connections with mothers of children the same age.

Eating together is one of the most obvious daily expressions of the group dynamic in action. I'm still touched by the looks of pity from my students when an awkward class schedule occasionally obliges me to eat lunch alone, as even the most harried Korean is likely to find time to eat a quick meal with a colleague, classmate or friend. Many dishes are shared, and this basic assumption even trickles into single portions of foreign foods: many times have I stopped for a treat after a solo shopping trip and been handed one ice cream sundae and two spoons.

One also sees the group ethos expressed in language use, like the abundant use of the pronoun *uri* ("we/us"). *Uri* is one of those words that, upon learning it, one suddenly seems to hear everywhere: in references to the Korean language (*urimal*, "our language"), to Korea itself (*uri nara*, "our country"), in the names of companies (Woori Bank) and even in cases where a first person pronoun seems the more logical choice, as in the way Korean wives are able to refer to their spouses as *uri nampyeon* ("our husband") without even the slightest suggestion of polygamy.

Another manifestation of the group ethos is in the tendency to value conformity over non-conformity. Though the iconoclasts and oddballs are beginning to gain acceptance as Korea strives to encourage a more creative economy, it is still true that Koreans are often obliged to meet group expectations in some way or another. Different people will experience this differently, especially people from the West, where an ideal liberal arts education has long emphasised the critical examination of authority and received wisdom. Many Koreans also experience conformity as a stifling experience that suppresses individual desires and new ideas, while also valuing the sword's double edge, as it provides a reliable set of guidelines to help navigate social situations and achieve group solidarity.

Though this general disposition toward grouping together is manifest in many ways, it is also riding alongside an increasingly apparent tendency toward individualism, as younger Koreans more often march to the beat of their own drums. Some indicators of the shift on the family level are the decline in marriage rates, the rise of divorce rates and the increased desire to live with one's nuclear family as opposed to the extended-family households that were more common even a generation ago. Many younger Koreans no longer wait for marriage to move out on their own, and in recent years, single households have become the most common type of living arrangement (27%), ahead of two-person (26%) and four-person households (19%). Even the taboo against eating alone for fear of looking like an outcast has diminished in the age of hectic schedules and Instagram food pics, and many restaurants that would not have served solo diners in the past are now opening their doors and scaling down portions to accommodate this new *honbap* ("rice for one person") trend.

RUDENESS

Rude people exist in every society on Earth in roughly the same proportions, yet one sometimes hears foreigners complain that "Koreans are rude", and they will point to various behaviours as evidence: letting doors close on the folks behind them, bumping into each other in public without excusing themselves, disrespecting the queue, asking probing questions about age and marital status, and on and on and on.

To be sure, there are rude people in Korea, and many Koreans will be more than happy to point this out to you and rail about it at length. But it's essential to bear in mind that whether or not a particular behaviour is rude depends not only on who is doing what to whom, but where, and that behaviours considered rude in one country's cultural context are not necessarily rude in another. Filling your own wine glass wouldn't raise an eyebrow at a dinner party in Vancouver, but doing the same in Seoul might draw a chiding comment or embarrass your Korean host for his inattentiveness. Addressing your British manager by his or her first name may signal friendly informality, but in Korea it is unambiguously condescending and would be grounds for immediate dismissal. Sometimes we may even agree that a behaviour is wrong, but disagree on the severity of the offence, as when Bill Gates shook hands with President Park Geun-hye in 2013 with his left hand in his pocket. While many Americans chided Mr Gates for what they considered a minor lapse in etiquette, most Koreans perceived it as a grave insult and a blow to national dignity.

By the same token, some of the things that are considered rude in Western countries may carry little or no stigma in Korea. Nudging your way past someone on a Korean subway car or brushing past them on a sidewalk is an inconsequential and unremarked feature of the average Korean's daily life, but to many Western newcomers, taught by their cultural upbringing to "respect other people's space" (and who likely had a fair bit more space to work with), a simple act like this strikes them as anything from an annoyance to an affront worthy of a newspaper editorial or Facebook rant.

In dealing with these kinds of trespasses on our cultural sensibilities, it's helpful to recall that to claim someone is "rude" is to say that he or she has violated social norms—the spoken and unspoken consensus by which every society defines acceptable behaviour. To say then that the *general* behaviour of most people *in their own country* is "rude" makes no sense on its face, because what one is saying in effect is that the local consensus has both settled on a proper mode of conduct and then universally chosen to flout it. To be sure, you'll encounter rude people in Korea from time to time, but if it happens that nearly every person you meet, day in and day out, appears to be acting "rudely", it's worth pausing to ask yourself whether it's more likely that you have simply misunderstood the local norms and are substituting your own as the benchmark.

Another common assumption that leads many expats to hand-wringing and grief is the idea that because modern cities now share many structural features, they should all more or less behave the same way; as if by constructing escalators, supermarket checkouts, roundabouts, sidewalks, elevators, subways and cell phones, one is also bundling them with a universal code of conduct that should be both readily apparent and universally adopted by users wherever they be; and if it is not, it should be taken as a wilful lapse of civility or lack of common sense. To be fair, some norms became norms because they represent an objectively good way of doing something: for example, letting people get off a crowded subway car before you attempt to get on is not merely good etiquette, it's good physics. But very often the norms we are accustomed to—like holding a door open for someone three metres behind you or leaving the toilet seat up (or is it supposed to be down?)—are merely expressive of a cultural preference that could just as easily have been otherwise, and are in fact different in other countries.

Like all modern societies, Korea's customs and etiquette are forever playing catch-up to technological and social changes, and the same lag is still readily apparent in Western countries, as our numerous advice columns, blogs, and letters to the editor attest. Rules for social interaction are no longer carved on stone tablets, but are continually discussed, debated, defined and refined until a rough consensus emerges. One can easily observe this process in real time whenever a new gadget hits the market, and even for many years after. At this writing, cell phones have been in common use for over thirty years; yet a Google search for "cell phone etiquette" turns up nearly 300 entries published *just in the past month*, including one rather worryingly titled "13 Ways You're Being Rude with Your Device (and Don't Even Know It!)". Korea is no different in this game of catch-up; if anything, the lag may often seem more pronounced, as they started from further behind technologically and progressed much faster, shifting from overwhelmingly rural to overwhelmingly urban in the space of two generations.

There's another strain of expat thinking that tends to overestimate the commonality of "common" sense, and claims that despite this rate of change and lack of precedent, the preference for certain behaviours should be immediately obvious to anyone. Thus, by not adopting them, one is being willingly dense, stubborn or—here's that word again—rude. While there may be objectively good reasons for queuing to the side of a subway car door or not stopping in the middle of an intersection in heavy traffic, these types of mutually beneficial group behaviours are not necessarily self-evident and in fact may often be counter-intuitive, as they often oblige us to put aside what appears to be our immediate self-interest (getting on a train quickly; not getting caught at a red light) in favour of a less apparent but greater long-term benefit (not being inconvenienced by millions of other people blocking train doors and intersections). Regardless of one's feelings about a particular issue, the good news is that when public education campaigns or some other type of enforcement make the new rules clear, Koreans have no trouble following them, and *voila*, the "rudeness" disappears.

Everyone knows that when in Rome, it is wise to do as the Romans do, but that's not to say you will like the new normal or that you should necessarily start emulating those behaviours that bother you (though I admit to feeling an enjoyable mix of guilt and liberation when I adopted the local custom of nudging other people's shopping carts out of my way in Costco). In the same spirit, learn to take your cues from locals on how to react in the face of a perceived slight. If everyone around you seems to be taking certain things in stride, you may ultimately be doing yourself a favour by learning to do the same.

ATTITUDES TOWARD HOMOSEXUALITY

Some older Koreans will occasionally tell you that there were no homosexuals in Korea in the past and that they have only recently appeared, probably as a result of liberal Western influences. While it's of course not true that hundreds of thousands of Korean heterosexuals have undergone a media-induced flipping of their sexual orientation, it is true that today's increased visibility of Korean LGBT people is more likely just a sign of the country's increasing acceptance of them, and of the greater confidence many LGBT folks have in living more openly.

Traditionally, Koreans have held marriage and family as high priorities, which left little room for homosexuals in the social order. A son was supposed to continue the family line, and women were supposed to get married and bear children, so a homosexual son or daughter would have been considered an unmitigated disaster. Gay men of older generations almost without exception got married and raised families, and lived closeted or double lives.

Today, many cultural, social and economic factors have conspired to weaken the formerly ironclad imperative to marry and multiply. High costs have put marriage and children out of reach for some people, young women are better educated and are more often choosing to pursue careers, and increased rates of divorce among middle-aged Koreans have made them less likely to push their kids into marrying for its own sake. The upshot is that remaining single indefinitely is now an option for many young Koreans across the board, which has also reduced the pressure on gay men and lesbians to use marriage as a cover.

Opinions in the LGBT community regarding the degree of discretion required are mixed. Some prefer to keep their orientation to themselves, as certain segments of society still view homosexuality quite negatively. Among younger Koreans however, a more tolerant and accepting attitude seems to be more common, and many younger gays and lesbians are more likely to be out than was the case even a few years ago.

XENOPHOBIA

Since ancient times, Koreans have looked outward for inspiration and absorbed a variety of influences from their neighbours, but their occasional rough treatment at the hands of foreign powers has also taught them to be wary of outsiders in their midst (including their allies), a defensive stance that earned Joseon-era Korea the moniker "The Hermit Kingdom".

The old us-against-the-world mentality hasn't entirely disappeared, but an independent, prosperous and increasingly confident Korea today finds itself engaged and intertwined with the world like never before, and has a foreign population of around 4%, roughly a tenfold increase from two decades earlier, and which has doubled since 2007. Though this small minority does not yet make Korea a true multicultural society, all signs are pointing in that direction, as increasing numbers of immigrants weave themselves into the social fabric.

Younger Koreans tend to show the greatest openness to all things foreign. Years of asking Korean undergrads, "Have you ever travelled abroad?" in our lessons on the present perfect tense has revealed that overseas travel is no longer the rarity it was when I arrived in 1998. Ten per cent of all weddings in Korea now involve a foreigner, and Koreans who marry foreigners today are much more likely to be envied than admonished, as was true in the past. Foreign food trends find the most fertile ground in university districts, whence they ripple outward.

This is not to say that Korea is immune from xenophobia on the national level, or that foreign individuals no longer experience racial or ethnic bias. Many businesspeople report feeling a sense that they are not as trusted as a Korean would be in the same position. From time to time, one will hear of a bar or nightclub banning foreigners, read a news story that sensationalises crime committed by foreigners (when in fact they are statistically less likely to break the law), or hear of a nosy passer-by who attempts to "rescue" a Korean woman from a foreign companion who turns out to be her boyfriend or husband, as happened to me outside a nightclub years ago as I was trying to assist my wobbly fiancée into a cab.

Such xenophobic outbursts get a lot of airtime in the foreign community, but are increasingly the exception to the rule and are greatly outnumbered by the expressions of goodwill and help offered by Koreans to foreigners, another notable tendency to which most foreign residents will readily attest. Far from considering you a menace, the majority of Koreans tend to either leave you in peace or will consider it "nice to meet you".

CHAPTER 4

SOCIALISING AND FITTING IN

‛Tradition is a guide and not a jailer.’

— W Somerset Maugham

HOW KOREANS SEE YOU

In past decades, foreigners were more of a rarity in Korea. Today, one has to go pretty deep into the sticks to find a Korean who has never met a foreigner, and expatriates who used to complain that they were treated as a spectacle are now more likely to complain of their anonymity.

Because of Korea's long association with US soldiers, volunteers, missionaries and businesspeople, there was a time when most Koreans of a certain age assumed that all Westerners in their country were Americans, but this is no longer the default assumption. While it's true that Americans are still a sizable part of the foreign population, many years of experience with other foreigners (and many touchy reactions from people who have been misidentified as Americans) have successfully conveyed the message that Korea's foreign community hails from around the world. As a result, the question, "Are you American?" has been replaced as the most common icebreaker by the more open-ended, "Where you are from?"

Lifelong Seoul resident Peter Underwood recalls how in the 1960s, when Korea was in the early stages of its economic development, Americans and Europeans were "put on a pedestal" and that many Koreans were like second-class citizens in their own country. "Foreigners were all *kap* at that time," he says, using the Korean term that describes the senior party in a hierarchical social relationship. This is no longer the case, as Korea's economic and cultural rise has brought with it a more palpable sense of confidence and national pride. While it's true that foreigners sometimes report varying degrees of prejudice, especially darker-skinned expats and labourers from South Asia, Koreans generally treat foreigners with respect, and tend to be flattered that people of other countries find Korea to be a desirable place to live and work.

BEING KOREAN

Korean identity has both a national and ethnic component. As such, even foreigners who have acquired Korean citizenship, speak Korean fluently and have acculturated in every way possible (including some who were born and raised here) will never be seen as completely Korean.

There are positives and negatives to this. To some, this permanent outsider status is the deal-breaker that prevents them from feeling truly integrated and/or comfortable living in Korea long term, no matter how much they may love the country otherwise. However long they stay, they will always be a *waegukin* (foreigner), and they often express a desire to ultimately settle in a place where they can be a fully participating and integrated member of society.

To others, this role of permanent outsider is a relatively minor issue that is partly compensated by a concomitant lack of duties and demands that full participation in society entails (observance of holiday rituals, unflagging attention to social obligations, military conscription, etc). Though I admit I occasionally find it strange that I have now lived in Korea long enough to regularly be referred to as a "foreigner" by Koreans who had not yet been born when I arrived here, my foreigner status has had no meaningful negative impact on my lifestyle, happiness and general satisfaction with life, and there are thousands of other foreign residents for whom the positives far outweigh whatever negatives they experience.

Many foreign residents will also attest that they are often the beneficiaries of special treatment and consideration, whether it's an offer of help at the post office, or an offer of a job teaching English, even when one's only qualifications are a college degree in anything and a willingness to give it a go, as has been the case for the past couple of decades for thousands of young Westerners. The fact that many of us settled in Korea at all is itself testament to a wholesale policy of preferential treatment that more often has worked in our favour.

Perhaps because of the ethnic nature of Korean identity, many Koreans assume that many aspects of Korean culture—from food to language to social norms—are inscrutable or impenetrable to outsiders. Sometimes these assumptions are fair, and sometimes they're overstated, but true or not, the upshot is that it tends to set the bar quite low for foreigners who wish to assimilate, and makes the average Korean relatively tolerant of the odd faux pas or cross-cultural gaffe.

This blanket cultural amnesty, lovingly referred to by Korea's expat community as "The Dumb Foreigner Card" can be both a nuisance and a boon, but it should not be understood as a license to act as one pleases. There are some basic rules that you need to observe, others that you are wise to observe and still others that you will scarcely be expected to know about that will earn you goodwill for observing. Reputations are built on an accumulation of small acts, and sincere effort seldom goes unnoticed.

Kibun, Nunchi and Chemyeon

To better understand and navigate Korean social interactions, it's helpful to recall that the main thrust of the Confucian tradition was to create a harmonious society, and that toward that end, Confucian thinkers stressed the importance of human relationships. As the descendants of that tradition, modern Koreans still find many of those same impulses informing their interactions with their families, communities and organisations, and employ a well-articulated set of principles that centre around some fundamental concepts.

One concept that is important to reckon with straight away is the Korean notion of *kibun*. *Kibun* doesn't have a precise translation into English, but it encompasses the idea of a person's mood, feelings, pride or current state of mind, so to say that one's *kibun* is good ("*kibuni joayo*") is to say that the self is at a harmonious equilibrium—that one enjoys a sense that all is currently right with one's social world.

To lower someone's *kibun* is to hurt them in a way that goes a bit deeper than what we mean when we say we "hurt someone's feelings" or put them "in a bad mood". There are many ways to damage someone's *kibun*: addressing someone the wrong way, using excessively informal language or inadvertently insulting them (for example by speaking negatively of their hometown or university), will all do the trick, and may result in anything from temporary awkwardness to a terminal break in a relationship.

> Having a quick sense of *nunchi* can help with knowing when to ask for a favour, gauging the right time to deliver bad news, knowing when to offer one's unvarnished opinion, when to sugarcoat and when to change the subject.

Given the potential social costs, the ability to read the *kibun* of others is an important skill. This ability, called *nunchi* (literally "eye measure") is especially important, because while Koreans may sometimes wear their hearts on their sleeves, many other social contexts require them to keep their thoughts and feelings to themselves, which in turn places the onus on the observer to be able to read them.

The concept of *chemyeon*, analogous to the Western notion of "face", is another important factor in managing Korean social relationships. Like the physical face you present to the world, *chemyeon* refers to the social standing you claim and represent to society, and it thus comes with certain obligations, both to you in acknowledging the status of others and treating them accordingly, and to others when interacting with you. Any behaviour that denies or minimises that self-image may result in what we call "losing face"; while "saving face" describes the effort to act in a way that acknowledges, respects, or salvages someone's social position.

Many social considerations flow from this very basic principle. It is to save face that one refrains from criticising or disagreeing with a superior directly even when you are sure that they are wrong, and takes care to express disagreement even with peers in a ginger, roundabout way. Koreans often take great pains to preserve face, as a loss of face can have severe repercussions: poisoned

One consequence of the face-saving impulse is that Korea has very strict libel/defamation laws, which can land you in trouble for public comments that damage a person's reputation, *even if the statement is entirely true*. As you would expect, many journalists, both foreign and Korean, chafe under such laws, which, perhaps unsurprisingly, have often been used to suppress even fair criticism that serves the public interest.

relationships, scotched business deals, and in extreme cases in which face has been irretrievably lost, to suicide.

INTERACTING WITH KOREANS

Though Korea has a larger international profile than it did even a few years ago, Koreans still generally expect foreigners to not know very much about Korea or Korean culture, and will often express surprise when someone utters a simple greeting in Korean, expresses a love of kimchi or recites a few basic facts about Korean history. The flipside of this occasional astonishment at your most basic cultural competencies is that Koreans also tend to be very forgiving of mistakes. Thus, rather than be annoyed at the 100th person who marvels at your ability to use chopsticks, it's worth reminding yourself that the spirit motivating that comment is the very same assumption that has probably already forgiven you a hundred cultural faux pas and minor transgressions.

When interacting with Koreans, whether in an official capacity or an informal exchange, patience, good humour and a smile go a long way. An attitude of humility is also more in line with the Korean way, and will get you much farther than a hard-charging, no-nonsense approach. When problems arise, try to let your first assumption be that people are not out to get you; which is not to say that some people are not bona fide jerks, only that the vast majority are not, and that sincere misunderstandings are a common occurrence in cross-cultural settings. Above all, do your best to avoid showing anger. Some foreigners find that raising their voice and causing a scene occasionally gets results, but it's important to understand while it may push some people to offer a quick solution just to be rid of the angry foreigner, it also marks you as a person not to be dealt with and will carry social repercussions.

Meeting People

Koreans tend not to approach strangers and introduce themselves and instead prefer to be introduced by a third party. Introductions are important in Korea: to be introduced to someone is to have the beginning of a social relationship, and all relationships in Korea place demands and responsibilities on both parties. For this reason, you may find that when you bump into Koreans you know on the street, they often will not introduce you to the person they happen to be with unless it is someone close to them like a spouse or sibling. They don't do this to be rude, but out of consideration: they don't want to unnecessarily burden either of you with the demands of a formal introduction unless there's a compelling reason to do so.

When being introduced to someone, Koreans say, "*Cheoeum poepgaessumnida*," ("This is the first time to see [you]"). If the introduction occurs in a work or business setting, business cards will be exchanged (more on that in Chapter 9: Working in the Country).

Despite the preference for personal introductions, as a foreigner in Korea, you'll probably find that Koreans will nonetheless approach you sometimes to chat. Some are trying out their English, which until then had been limited to a classroom. Others have lived or travelled abroad and enjoy meeting and talking to people from overseas, as I am often drawn to Koreans when I meet them in my travels. And others

Koreans also tend to ask many personal questions when meeting someone for the first time (age, marital status, hometown, alma mater, etc.) both to quickly establish relative status (which is an important factor in determining the type of language they must use), and to find points of commonality.

are just trying to be friendly or helpful, especially if you appear to be lost or having some kind of difficulty. Many Koreans sincerely want foreigners in their country to have a positive experience and a good impression of Korea, and you will sometimes find random strangers doing things for you that may be hard to imagine happening in big cities elsewhere: sharing an umbrella, offering to translate for you, walking you to your destination instead of merely explaining it, and sometimes even offering directions rather than say they don't know where something is, as when I once asked two women the way to a particular temple, to which they simultaneously responded by pointing in opposite directions.

Bowing

Koreans perform a simple bow in many social situations, like meeting someone, bidding farewell or expressing thanks. The depth of the bow reflects greater respect, though a slight bend at the waist will usually suffice for most common situations. Directing one's gaze downward is also considered polite, as eye contact doesn't carry the same connotation of honesty or attentiveness as it does in Western countries and can be considered rude in certain contexts.

It may feel awkward at first, but bowing eventually becomes second nature. Many Westerners who have spent a long time in Korea even find themselves instinctively bowing to friends and family back in their home countries.

A deep bow, called *sebae*, is the greatest physical display of respect and deference, and is reserved for occasions

like *jesa* (ancestral rites), funerals and certain holidays like *Seollal* (Lunar New Year), when young Koreans bow to their parents and grandparents. Performing a *sebae* involves getting into a kneeling position, placing ones clasped hands on the floor in front of you, and bowing so that your forehead touches the floor and remains there for a few seconds, before standing up.

A Seoul statue demonstrates proper form for bowing in greeting.

Most Koreans today also shake hands when meeting someone, though it is also accompanied by a short bow. A polite handshake employs two hands, either by clasping the right arm at the elbow with the left hand or by placing the left hand on the sternum. To show real warmth and pleasure to see someone, clasp his or her hand with both of yours.

GENERAL ETIQUETTE
Giving and Receiving
In general, the polite way to receive something, whether it be a business card, a pair of chopsticks, or an envelope, is to use two hands, either by grasping the object itself with two hands, or by receiving it with the right while supporting the right arm below the elbow with the left. When handing something to someone, the same rules apply. If you are giving or receiving something from someone younger or of lower status, use one hand, as two hands is excessively deferential.

Beckoning
To gesture someone to come to you, extend your arm forward with the palm facing down and make a waving motion downward and toward yourself. To brush someone off, Koreans start from the same position but wave the hand upward instead. Beckoning someone with one finger is considered rude or even aggressive. The Western style of beckoning (waving toward yourself with your palm facing you) is how Koreans fan themselves on hot days when the A/C isn't working.

Eye Contact
Unlike some Western cultures where eye contact is considered to be a sign of honesty or attentiveness, eye contact in Korea may be considered rude when it is directed toward an older person, especially one who is reprimanding you. If someone is looking downward while you are speaking to them, he or she is more likely showing deference, not being evasive.

Queuing
Koreans queue in the same types of settings that are recognisable to foreigners (for example at elevators, checkout

counters, by the sides of subway car doors, etc) but may apply it much more loosely (or not at all) in other places, like traditional markets or at street food carts. When one does see a queue jumper in a setting where queuing is the norm, it is almost always a much older person who has one foot squarely in the old country. Occasionally Koreans will say something to the offender, but often they let it go, particularly if he or she is quite old.

Door Holding

One doesn't go out of one's way in Korea to hold doors open for people you do not know, however many younger Koreans appear to be picking up this habit, perhaps as a result to travelling and picking up foreign customs in Europe, North America and Australia. For many Westerners, this common nicety is deeply ingrained and is often enshrined in our notions of what constitutes "gentlemanly" or "civilised" behaviour in our respective cultures. If people don't hold doors for you, bear in mind that it is because Korean social etiquette does not currently create that particular obligation (though it may in the future if current trends persist), not because they are breaking with an established code of proper conduct. If you're like me, you may find yourself instinctively holding doors open despite their being no repercussion whatsoever for not doing so, but be prepared not to get bent out of shape if you don't receive any acknowledgement.

Smoking

Smoking is still fairly common but is rapidly becoming more restricted. Traditionally there has been a taboo against women smoking, and women do still occasionally report dirty looks or comments, particularly from middle-aged or elderly men. Be aware that many buildings now prohibit smoking within a certain distance of the entrance, and that these rules are often enforced.

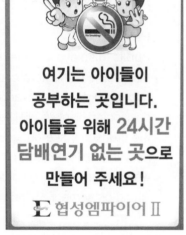

A sign in my neighbourhood appeals to children's health in asking smokers to create a 24-hour smoke-free zone.

Giving Up a Seat

It used to be common for younger people to give up their seats on the bus or subway for elderly passengers, but the fact is that it's a dying custom and is now only a habit of the older generation, who unfortunately are the ones who should be getting the seats, not giving them up. As a response, many cities have started reserving seating for elderly, handicapped and pregnant passengers—these are the seats nearest the doors and are clearly marked with signs and different colouring. Giving up your seat unbidden seems no longer to be required and will probably not be a faux pas if you don't, though doing so is certainly appreciated and sets a good example for nearby whippersnappers.

Blowing Your Nose in Public

Avoid blowing your nose in public, especially at the table. Try as much as possible to do it discretely, or remove yourself to the bathroom if you really need to "clean house".

PDA

Public displays of affection are much more subdued than in many Western countries. For Westerners, a hello/goodbye kiss or hug is accepted and understood, but more passionate displays will likely draw negative attention—even the drunken make-out session in bars or clubs is relatively rare. In public, Koreans are physically expressive in other ways, for example by holding hands, clasping the waist, or sitting on someone's lap.

Same-sex friends have more freedom for physical contact than heterosexuals are permitted in most Western countries, and it's thus still common to see women walking hand-in-hand or with linked arms, and men draping their arms over each other's shoulders as they walk, or resting a hand on a friend's leg as they talk over a beer. Homosexual couples report that engaging in the same type of contact with their significant others in public usually passes entirely unremarked.

Gift-giving

Gifts are given for a variety of reasons in Korea: on certain holidays, birthdays, weddings, as a thank you to staff or as a way of establishing good relations with a client. If the gift is an item of some kind, always have it gift-wrapped (most Korean shops will do this for you free of charge). When receiving a gift, it should not be opened in front of the giver. It is also considered polite for Koreans to initially refuse a gift once or twice before agreeing to accept it. Not engaging in this ritual back and forth can make one appear to be greedy.

Cash gifts should always be given in an envelope; handing someone cash directly as a gift is considered tacky and rude. Many convenience stores sell envelopes for this purpose, and many will have envelopes for specific occasions, like weddings and funerals.

At Home

Koreans generally don't throw parties at home, but they do occasionally have a few guests over for dinner, coffee, and other small gatherings; thus, being invited to someone's house is generally a bigger deal than it is elsewhere. If someone invites you for an informal get-together, bringing a bottle of wine, some flowers, or a box of fruit will be fine. A small exception is the housewarming party, or *jipdeuri*, in which Koreans invite many people over to eat, drink and be merry in the new digs. If you are invited to one, it's common to bring a small gift for the house, like bathroom tissue, a house plant, a clock or laundry detergent.

Never enter the main part of the house with your shoes on. Even the humblest of Korean homes has a small vestibule where guests remove their shoes. Also remember to heed your mother's advice not to wear socks with holes unless you're okay with everyone seeing them.

If you are the host, be prepared to make a lot of good food, as that is what your guests would do in the reverse situation. After the meal, it's common to talk and linger over a drink or two (or four, or six), but remember to put out some kind of light food or snack, like nuts, cookies, fruit, dried squid, chips and dip, cheese, etc. The general rule is to have some kind of food available to your guests at all times, otherwise you may be signalling that the party's over.

As far as what to cook, note that most Koreans today are familiar with and fond of many foreign foods, and are generally open to trying new things, especially something you have gone out of your way to prepare. To be safe, you may want to provide something Korean for the pickier eaters. A little kimchi is never out of place.

Most Koreans are comfortable sitting on the floor for extended periods, though these days most Korean homes are also furnished with tables and chairs. If entertaining at your own home, your guests will likely be fine with either arrangement. For floor seating, thin cushions are a nice touch. Some people also use floor seats with back support (picture a contoured wooden chair with no legs), for those of us who find it hard to sit cross-legged comfortably for very long.

Be mindful of your guests' glasses and offer to fill them when they are empty, but not before. Leaving a glass partly full is a way of signalling that you've had enough to drink.

Ice cream and cakes constitute dessert for some people today, but fruit tends to be more popular, and is best when it is in season. Supermarkets often have a variety of imported fruit (pineapple, mango, kiwi, etc) and these too go over well.

At the end of the night, Korean guests tend to leave all at

once, regardless of whether they came together. A proper send-off is to walk them out to their car or taxi and bid farewell outside.

SOCIAL FUNCTIONS
Weddings
There's some variation in weddings, but most these days take place in a "wedding hall", which is usually attached to a buffet-style restaurant, and will often have several ceremonies taking place one after the other in an almost assembly-line fashion: greet the family, attend the ceremony, pose for pictures, eat and go home. On entering, it's standard practice to leave a cash gift in an envelope (which is usually provided there) with your name on the back and a word or two of congratulations on the front. Fifty-thousand won in crisp, new banknotes is the norm for a casual acquaintance; for someone who works with you or with whom you have a closer relationship, it's common to give more.

Modern Korean weddings have incorporated many of the trappings and traditions of Western weddings: the groom wears black, the bride wears white and an esteemed figure who knows the family (like a professor, judge or high-ranking member of one's company) officiates and gives a speech that nobody but the couple seems to listen to. Immediately following the ceremony, there is a round of photos including family and guests, so you may want to stick around for a few more minutes to pose with the happy couple. Dress is formal, but not overly so; business casual will do.

Modern weddings also incorporate elements of traditional Korean weddings, particularly in the deep bows performed by the bride and groom to the parents and soon-to-be in-laws. The bride and groom will also usually change into

The wedding cake is another cultural import that seems to have caught on.

traditional wedding outfits after the ceremony for a round of photos before heading out to the banquet room. The Korean love of song may also be on display, as another common feature of contemporary weddings is to have a friend of the couple sing a song, and hope that countless hours of *noraebang* crooning finally pays off.

Many couples also like to put their own fun spin on their nuptials, as in one recent wedding I attended that featured a *Star Wars* theme and a dancing entrance procession set to pumping dance music. At the recent wedding of my wife's niece, the best man instructed the groom to run around the room with his shoe in his hand to collect money in order to "see who his real friends are". He dashed down the rows while guests stuffed 10,000-won notes in his shoe, after which he ran back to the altar, dumped his haul into a basket, and was told by the best man to hand it over to his wife and to "get used to it".

Traditional weddings are increasingly rare, and are ironically practiced more often by foreigners who wed in Korea and want a "Korean" experience; of the half dozen or so traditional weddings I've attended in Korea, they were in every case either a wedding between a foreigner and a Korean or two foreigners. Traditional wedding ceremonies are often held in open courtyard settings, and feature colourful outfits, rich symbolism and elaborate bows offered to the families of the bride and groom. If you are invited to one, you can observe the same general etiquette as for a contemporary-style wedding.

Baekil Janchi (100-day Party)

For most of human history, infant mortality rates were high, so a baby surviving those first crucial weeks and months was indeed a thing to celebrate. In Korea, the baby was traditionally kept at home for the first few months, and finally brought out at the *baekil janchi* (100-day party) as both a celebration of life as well as the child's first introduction to the kin. These days, though infant mortality rates have plummeted to first-world levels, the *baekil janchi* is still celebrated in Korea, and is usually held in a banquet room or buffet, where a big meal is served, and friends and relatives compliment the parents and fawn over the new arrival.

If you are invited to a *baekil janchi*, dress formally and bring a gift. Close relatives often give a gold ring, which was a form of insurance for the family in older times. For friends or acquaintances, baby clothes or an age-appropriate toy will work, or if it is someone close to you, a silver chopstick and spoon set is a common gift. Be prepared to stay for a while, eating and drinking with the new parents and friends.

Ddol Janchi (First Birthday)

The first birthday party, called *ddol janchi*, is also celebrated in Korea, and along with the 60th birthday is considered one of the milestone years. The *ddol janchi* is similar to the *baekil janchi* but is generally a bigger event.

At the *ddol janchi*, the child wears a colourful *hanbok* (traditional outfit) and occupies a central place in the banquet room along with his or her parents. Apart from eating and socialising, one of the main events is the *doljabi* ceremony, in which a variety of objects are placed on a table in front of the child, and predictions about the child's future are made depending on which one he or she reaches for.

The objects vary, but they often include money (symbolising future wealth), thread (symbolising long life), a pen (which indicates a future scholar), a microphone (entertainer), a gavel or a stethoscope. Parents will often rig the placement of the objects to encourage the selection of the more auspicious tokens—usually the money.

Invitations to first birthday parties often go out by word of mouth and on short notice. If you are invited, do try to attend. It's an honour to attend, and is a good chance to enjoy one of Korea's oldest customs, to deepen bonds with Korean friends and colleagues and to sample some excellent traditional and contemporary cuisine. If your child has a first birthday in Korea, throwing a *ddol janchi* a good excuse to invite your Korean friends and workmates to a party, though as a foreigner, there is no expectation for you to do so and no one will fault you for celebrating in the manner of your choosing.

Hwangap (60th Birthday Party)

The *hwangap* (60th birthday party) has also been a cause for celebration, as it traditionally represented the last major milestone in life. At a *hwangap*, the guest of honour is given a large feast or fancy meal, during which members of the family pay respects in various ways. The more elaborate parties will feature singing and dancing in a large banquet room, while the more low-key celebrations may comprise toasts and speeches around a table of fine food with a few members of the immediate family.

Like many traditions, the *hwangap* too is changing with the times. Alongside Korea's economic development, life expectancy has likewise risen dramatically, from an average of 52 years in 1960 to over 82 years today. Not surprisingly, this has taken some of the shine off of the *hwangap*, and many Korean families are forgoing the occasion and celebrating the 70th birthday with a big party instead. Perhaps future generations will establish traditions around the 100th birthday, but for now, 70 seems to be the new 60.

Funerals

In the unfortunate event you need to attend a funeral, black, formal attire is a must. Most funerals are held in *jangnaesikjang* (funeral parlours) that are almost always attached to hospitals. Depending on your relationship with the family, you may be required to perform a bow in front of a photo of the deceased, which involves facing the photo, dropping to both knees and bowing down so that your forehead touches the floor for a few seconds. Just to be safe, I've made it a personal rule never to be the first to rise; if you're on your own, a count of "five-Mississippi" will suffice. It's also customary to perform a standing bow at the waist to the family of the departed.

Funeral guests are also invited to partake in a light meal in a separate area of the funeral parlour that will likely include a drink or two of beer or *soju*. Feel free to indulge, but note that the mood is much more sombre than the typical Korean drinking session, and that toasting or clinking glasses should be avoided.

Typically, Koreans give a cash gift of 50,000 to 100,000 won to the family if the deceased was the relative of an acquaintance, and give larger amounts at funerals of those with whom (or with whose family) they are close.

TABOOS

Many Koreans will ask you what you think of Korea. It goes without saying that positive statements are preferred, and criticising the host's country anywhere is generally not received well, though this isn't to say it can't be done under certain circumstances. If your interlocutor has expressed his or her own negative opinion of some aspect of Korean life, you can agree without offending them (if you happen to agree), but shouldn't take it as a licence to open the floodgates.

If you do have a criticism you feel comfortable expressing, framing it in a constructive way or prefacing it with positive counterexamples will increase the odds of earning a sincere hearing and not being reflexively written off. The closer you are to Koreans, the more you will be privy to their own criticisms of their culture, society, political system, etc, and the more you will understand that they tend to have a far better understanding of those problems than the average foreign observer has or gives them credit for. Listen, learn and share your ideas and opinions, taking your conversational cues from the social context.

Sex is a touchy subject for conversation in many cultures, and Koreans too tend to keep their sex lives to themselves, even among close friends. You may, however, be asked about your religious beliefs, though no one will fault you for saying you consider it personal. Discussing politics too can be tricky, as passions run high and feelings run deep. Better to feel out your listener first if you'd like to go there.

A few extra words of caution need to be said regarding the subject of Japan. Though Koreans are generally friendly to Japanese people and have many positive things to say about Japanese culture, they tend to have very negative feelings about Japan considered as a national entity, and they will often express anger and resentment at past wrongs and for what most Koreans feel has been the failure of former and current Japanese governments to redress them satisfactorily.

As a foreigner, there's no harm in expressing a love for Asahi beer or Japanese animation—indeed many Koreans will do the same—but referring to the Sea of Japan by anything other than its Korean name—the East Sea—will not be taken very well. Also note that South Korea and Japan are currently engaged in a territorial dispute over a Korean-controlled islet called Dokdo by Koreans and Takeshima by Japanese. Most third-party observers (including this author) agree that Korea has the far stronger claim, but if you happen to come to a different opinion, Korea is the last place in the world to air it.

Many social settings require Koreans to express disagreement obliquely or not at all, and they will almost never offer a flat rejection or contradiction of something that was said, especially by someone senior to them. Many foreigners have been flummoxed when a request that was apparently granted or a question that was answered affirmatively later turns out to have been negated. While many Westerners prefer a more direct style, be prepared nonetheless for answers that, though they may be intended to soften the blow, sometimes lead to confusion or bad feelings later on.

When you are the one expressing disagreement, be careful to do so in a way that doesn't come off as too strident, and avoid doing it in a group setting where you run the risk of causing a loss of face, especially when the person is senior to you. Choose your battles wisely, and be prepared to bite the bullet sometimes in the interest of maintaining a relationship, if it's one you wish to maintain.

Many foreign teachers complain that their students are passive, that they don't ask questions enough, or that they will claim to understand instructions which are later revealed to have been less than completely understood. Koreans have long subscribed to a teacher-centred approach to education, in which knowledge and information flows from teacher to student, who is expected to master the material. In such a system, questioning the teacher or expressing an alternate viewpoint was a no-no, and even claiming that one has not understood is often avoided, as it might be construed as an implication that the teacher failed to competently present the material. In short, one shouldn't assume that "I understand" means that the message was actually understood, and should make it a habit to check for confirmation in subtle ways (and to understand that "Repeat everything I just said" is not subtle). Some teachers have had success in cultivating a classroom culture in which students feel free to ask questions, but it's also good practice to create other opportunities, like after class or during office hours, for students to ask questions more comfortably.

For similar reasons, encouraging Korean work colleagues to offer constructive feedback can be tricky. If you'd like to create that sort of environment in your company or organisation, you will have to work to cultivate it. Asking for feedback tends to succeed best when it is accompanied by a preceding talk about why feedback is important to you, is structured in a way that asks specifically framed questions and is rewarded when offered. However you do it, the bottom line is not to take it for granted, or to take silence to mean that no one has any suggestions, complaints or ideas.

Bad Luck

Don't write someone's name in red pen or marker. According to some sources, red was the colour reserved for writing the names of the deceased during Buddhist memorial services, while others point out that the names of condemned prisoners were at one time inscribed in red ink. Still others have claimed

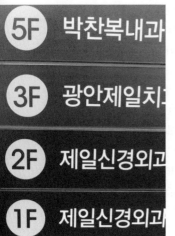

5F 박찬복내과

3F 광안제일치_

2F 제일신경외과

1F 제일신경외과

Many medical centres, like this one, opt to omit the fourth floor, as it can be a kiss of death to a doctor's practice.

that the taboo was imported long ago from the Chinese, who reserved red ink for the emperor, and thus viewed its use by anyone else as expressing contempt for his authority. Whatever the reason, Koreans today still consider it very bad form.

The number four is also considered bad luck in Korea, because the pronunciation (*sa*) sounds similar to the pronunciation of the Chinese character for "death". As a result, many buildings skip the fourth floor or replace the number on the elevator button with the letter "F", as this is apparently less likely to elicit the dreaded Chinese homophone. Bear this in mind if you're ever tempted to give four of anything as a gift, or a cash gift of 40,000 won.

CHAPTER 5

SETTLING IN

> ❝ By wisdom a house is built,
> And by understanding it is established. ❞

> — **Proverbs 24:3**

FINDING A HOME

Many companies, universities and *hagwons* will provide you with housing as part of your contract, often the former home of your predecessor. If you are house hunting in Korea on your own, one option is to visit a real estate agent or call one of the real estate agents who advertise on English-language sites. An advantage of going through an agent who caters to foreigners is that you can get a copy of your lease agreement in English as well as Korean; otherwise have a Korean friend or colleague help you understand the terms. Korean real estate agents tend to focus on one area, so visit a few real estate agents in areas that interest you and have them show you some places.

If you are trying to set up your move from outside Korea, a relocation company is another option. In addition to shipping services, some also provide help with house/apartment/office hunting, long-term storage, pet relocation, immigration/visa paperwork, among other services.

Renting

Houses and apartments are rented in one of two ways in Korea. *Jeonsae* (commonly called "key money") is a type of rental system in which the renter puts down a large, guaranteed deposit (in the neighbourhood of 50 per cent of the property's current market value), and then pays no monthly rent for the term of the lease, which is usually two years, after which the deposit is either refunded, or the lease is renegotiated and/or renewed.

These days, low interest rates are pushing many landlords to prefer the *wolsae* system, which is a system of monthly rent and a smaller initial deposit. Note that in the *wolsae* system, the size of the deposits are often negotiable, and have an inverse relationship to the amount of monthly rent charged, so paying a higher deposit can get you a cheaper monthly rate.

Korean housing units are measured in pyoung. One *pyoung* is approximately 3.3 sq m, or 35.5 sq ft.

Your rental agreement should also include clauses about repairs, termination of lease, utilities and subletting.

If you live in an apartment, your rental agreement will also stipulate a regular maintenance fee called *gwallibi*, which covers the cost of things like security, window cleaning, small repairs, etc.

Housing Types
Apateu (apartments)
Apartments are generally the largest and most expensive of the housing options available in Korea. Apartments have improved in the past couple of decades, transforming from identical concrete blocks to soaring glass and steel structures with better floor plans and various amenities including study rooms, laundry rooms, playgrounds, saunas, gyms, conference rooms and so on.

Though there has been a recent renewal of interest in houses, apartments are still the domicile of choice in Korea, and they are so closely associated with modernity and convenience that one even sees them far out in the countryside, where ample space would permit more spread-out development.

Doosan We've the Zenith Apartments in Busan, completed in 2011, are among the tallest residential buildings in the world. The tallest of the three has 80 floors and stands at 301 metres.

Jutaek (house)

Despite the popularity of apartment living, many people prefer houses for their lower prices and for not having neighbours literally on top of you. Houses also usually feature a small yard, which can be anything from a narrow slab of concrete with space for some planter boxes, to a broad patch of earth with ample space for gardening or barbecuing. In more cramped neighbourhoods, the *jutaek* roof functions as a virtual yard where people hang laundry, plant gardens, dry fish, squid or peppers, or sip a quiet beer at the end of the day.

Billa (villa)

Unlike the sprawling Tuscany estates that the name conjures, a "villa" in Korea refers to a walk-up apartment with anywhere from two to five floors. At one time, they were a luxury option, and while there are still some nice ones out there, they have somewhat fallen out of fashion. Villas are cheaper than apartments, and may be furnished or unfurnished.

Officetel

The word "officetel" is a compound of "office" and "hotel"; and while they are often used as small offices, their other use is actually as a residence, not a hotel. Officetels tend to be newer and fully furnished, though they are smaller than the average apartment, which tends to make them popular with single people and couples with no kids.

One-room

A step down in terms of size and price from the officetel, the "one-room" is usually partly furnished (desk, bed, small table), has built-in shelving and some closet space and a small kitchenette. Suitable for one person, or two people who get along extraordinarily well.

Gosiwon

These are the cheapest and smallest forms of accommodation, and are used mostly by students as a dormitory. They usually consist of not much more space than is necessary to lie down or sit at a desk, but if you only need it to sleep and cram for tests, it's a viable option that will only set you back around 200,000 won a month.

Furnishings

Many rental homes are either fully or partially furnished. For those that are not, a few options are available. If having your old furniture is important to you, you can have it shipped, though a better strategy might be to either liquidate your furniture when you move, or place it into cheap long-term storage if you anticipate moving back at some point.

New furniture can be purchased in various shops and department stores. Big stores like E-Mart, Home Plus and Costco are good options for getting your house set up, as they sell everything from frozen food to a refrigerator to keep it in, and also offer quick, cheap (and sometimes free) delivery. Ikea has also recently moved in, and offers much the same type of cheap, functional furniture they offer everywhere.

More Koreans are buying things online, as online retailers offer quick delivery (often next day) and have comparable or better prices to many of the big brick-and-mortar retailers. For setting up your house on the cheap, stores like Daiso sell many household items for 1,000 to 4,000 won, and can be a good place to get your no-frills coffee mugs, cutlery, dishes and such.

Second-hand shops (for furniture, appliances, etc) exist but are not as common, as Koreans tend to prefer new stuff. Foreign residents, who have fewer qualms about re-using old house wares, have created many informal exchanges of used goods online: Facebook groups and classified sections of local websites function as virtual yard sales, as people clear out their old furniture, bicycles, Tupperware and game consoles, while new arrivals cheaply furnish their new living spaces.

SHOPPING

Korea has a variety of shopping options, from small retail shops, to outdoor markets, to massive department stores. Every city has at least one shopping district, and Seoul has several. Many folks head to Hongdae or the area around Ehwa Women's University for clothing, shoes and accessories, Myoungdong for cosmetics and skin care products, and Dongdaemun market for pretty much anything.

Koreans and foreign residents alike are increasingly shopping online to get better deals or track down things that are otherwise hard or impossible to find. Many Korean sites have sprung up in recent years, and can be good places to find better prices on items that are available in retail shops. Some of the major sites, like Danawa, Naver, G-market and Ticketmonster are good places to start. Some are easier to navigate than others, but spending some time to get familiar with these and others can make shopping an all-around better experience in the long run.

The Shinsegae Department Store in Busan was certified in 2009 by the Guinness Book of World Records as the largest department store in the world.

Buying Korean

Depending on the product you are looking for, it will sometimes make more sense to favour a foreign brand, while in other cases the Korean brand will be the more logical choice. However, when all other factors are roughly equal, it pays to consider buying products from Korean companies, for one major reason: Korean companies score top marks when it comes to customer service and dealing with defective, broken or worn-out products, and they soundly out-perform foreign rivals in this regard. A trip to a local A/S Center almost always results in your item being fixed quickly and cheaply (sometimes even after the warrantee has expired), or in some cases, replaced outright with a new product.

WHAT TO BRING

There isn't much you need to bring to Korea in terms of material things, as most goods are available at reasonable prices. There are however a few things that many long-time residents find hard to track down or more cost-effective to bring with them or have shipped.

Spices

For goods that are unavailable in Korea, you may be better served by foreign sites like Amazon, which tend to have better prices on imports. Shop around and compare.

Common foreign spices like basil, curry powder, oregano, thyme and so on are usually available in Korean supermarkets. However, if you're into more esoteric flavours, stocking up on your preferred seasonings abroad is one way to make sure you have them on hand. Websites like iHerb have also been a godsend for getting those hard-to-procure spices.

Large Sizes

Outside of Seoul's Itaewon neighbourhood, which has long catered to tourists and US military personnel, the average Korean clothing or shoe store tends not to stock larger sizes. Note also that XL in Korea does not equate with the sizes labelled XL in the West, and anything larger than that is virtually unheard of. This applies to shoes larger than a US size ten, and brassieres larger than a C-cup.

Over-the-counter Medicines

Korean pharmacies are well-equipped to handle any bug that comes your way, but if there are specific brands of medicine (Deep Heat, Nyquil, etc.) that you prefer, you may be better off bringing them or having them sent to you. Also note that things like aspirin and antacid tablets tend not to

be sold in bulk sizes in Korean pharmacies, so stocking up on those outside of Korea can save you money and trips to the chemist.

Tampons

Tampons tend to be expensive, and many women report stocking up on those or having them shipped. Because of the expense, some recommend buying something reusable like a menstrual cup or sponge.

Apostilled Copies of Legal/Official Documents

Occasionally you will need to produce apostilled copies of official documents, and doing it before you come can save you time and money. Some documents to consider bringing extra apostilled copies of are your birth certificate, university diploma, marriage certificate and criminal background check.

Voltage Converter

If you bring your electronics and small electrical appliances, note that Korea's electricity runs at 220 volts, and the standard frequency is 60 Hz. If your home country is in the 220 to 240 volt range, they will work in Korea, but Americans and Canadians will need a voltage converter in order to use your 110-volt appliances. Voltage converters and plug adapters are cheaply available in electronics markets in cities around Korea.

Comfort Stuff

Embracing a new culture is part of the excitement of living abroad, but adjusting can be stressful, and many expats find it helpful to remain connected to the material culture of their home countries as a means of maintaining their identity, sanity and peace of mind. Whether it's a photo album, a treasured guitar or several tins of your favourite biscuit, it's often worth the effort to bring with you some of the things that make you feel at home.

TRANSPORTATION
Driving

To drive a car in Korea, you will need either an international driver's license or a Korean driver's license. Holders of a valid license from another country can obtain a Korean license fairly easily at a Korean Motor Vehicle Department (*Unjeon Myeonheo Siheomjang*). Bring your valid driver's license and passport, take a written test (in English), a brief eye exam and you'll soon be on your way.

For motorbikes, there are different license classes depending on the size of the bike. Scooters or street bikes under 125cc require a *wondonggi* license, while anything bigger requires the *ijongsohyoung* license. Both can

be acquired by visiting the nearest licensing agency, and many riders recommend going early to increase your odds of acquiring your new license the same day.

You can insure your vehicle through any insurance agency; some bigger companies like Samsung have dedicated English-speaking staff to guide you through the process and help you find a suitable coverage plan.

Dealing with Accidents

Car accidents are a frequent fact of life in Korea, and they are not adjudicated in quite the same way as what you may be used to. Liability is decided by taking into consideration not only the degree of fault, but which party suffered the most damage or incurred the greater loss. Therefore, an accident involving a law-abiding driver and a drunken, jay-walking pedestrian almost always results in a sizable payout for the latter. It is strongly recommended to get the most comprehensive insurance coverage you can afford.

One quirk of the Korean system is that there is no such thing as a hundred per cent fault, as a small degree of fault is assigned to even the most blameless and law-abiding of the two parties, apparently for no other reason than there would have been no accident at all if you had not been there. A lawyer friend of mine opines that it may also be a face-saving measure—a way of allowing the blameless party to soften the blow somewhat by accepting partial responsibility—even when the other party was clearly in the wrong, as was perhaps the case when he was judged to be 15 per cent at fault after being struck by a driver who had run a red light and made an illegal U-turn in a crosswalk while talking on a cell phone. Whatever the reason, if you find yourself on the relatively innocent end of the agreement, understand that a Korean in the same situation would also likely shoulder the same fault as you, and that even an 85 to 15 split in your favour will still result in you being compensated.

To avoid paying higher insurance rates, many Korean drivers also prefer to settle small scrapes and fender benders on the spot by negotiating a deal, exchanging a cash payment and leaving the insurance company and police out of it. This can often be a convenient and fair way to resolve small

accidents in which no one was hurt, and it may be worth the effort to try if you are involved in one. However, if someone has been injured, or if the terms of the deal offered by the other driver don't seem fair, it's better to go through the police and insurance company and have them hash it out.

On the Road

Though Korean society is orderly in many other ways, there are no Confucians on the roadways. Drivers must be simultaneously defensive and offensive, or as one acquaintance put it, the prevailing ethic is "the first one in gets the prize". Taxis may often be seen swerving to the curb to pick up fares, and even bus drivers may cross several lanes at once as they weave from stop to stop. Motorbike delivery drivers snake between slower moving cars, make liberal use of sidewalks when its more convenient (which it often is), and shoot the gaps between buses and the curb, occasionally adding an element of adventure to the otherwise mundane task of disembarking. Korean police aggressively enforce drunk driving laws and speeding infractions with random sobriety checkpoints, speed traps and stiff fines; but there are a host of other infractions that defy both the law and good sense that go either unnoticed or unregulated and will test both your abilities and your cool.

The Korean government has made efforts in the past few years to curb their high rates of motor vehicle accidents and traffic fatalities, which had been among the highest in the OECD. Initiatives like seat belt laws, school zone enforcement and traffic-light cameras appear to be bearing some fruit, and many of the worst metrics have shown slow but steady decline. While it's certainly not the Wild West, driving is neither the safest nor necessarily the fastest way to get around in Korea, especially in the city, where traffic can be hellish, parking can be difficult and/or expensive, and accidents both large and small are common. If you are a beginning driver or in any way uncomfortable behind the wheel, Korea is either not a good place to learn, or the ideal place to learn, depending on your point of view.

Opinions on whether to drive in Korea are mixed, but there is a rough consensus that if you anticipate doing most of your driving in the city, a car may be more trouble than it's worth. However, a car is a solid option for families with children and/or pets, for transporting cargo (camping gear, bicycles, bulk purchases from your monthly Costco run) and for regular excursions into the Korean countryside and getting to places that are otherwise hard to reach.

All modern apartment complexes these days provide dedicated parking for residents, but parking in the city can be challenging and you may often be obliged to park some distance from your destination. For street parking, the situation is changing in certain trouble spots, though one still finds that parking enforcement can be rather lax, and people will park, shall we say, creatively: double parking on main thoroughfares, creating bottlenecks by parking on both sides of narrow roads, or butting up against other parked cars. If you are a regular commuter by car, it's often a good idea to look into paying the monthly rate at a parking garage near your office or school.

Buying and Registering a Car

Many competitively-priced European and American car brands are available in Korea, though the majority of the cars on the road are Korean. Many Koreans and foreigners alike still opt to buy Korean cars for ease of repair and maintenance, competitive pricing and for their generally superior customer service. If you anticipate a lot of city driving, a smaller model will serve you well, as it will be much easier to park than an SUV or large sedan.

If you buy a new car, you can register it yourself at the registration in the district in which you live, or you can ask the dealer to do it for you (usually for a fee). To register, you will need to bring your ARC card and passport, proof of insurance, an inspection sticker, the temporary number plate and vehicle certificate issued by the dealer and the *jadongcha deungnok* (registration form). Cars must be registered within 15 days of purchase or face a fine.

When buying a used car, apart from asking the dealer for as much information about the car as possible, you should also visit the *gucheong* (District Office) where the car is currently registered to check if there are any outstanding taxes owed on the vehicle, and if all loans have been paid off. You can check for outstanding traffic fines on the vehicle online at etax.seoul.go.kr, though you may need a Korean-speaking friend or colleague to assist.

There are many companies that can insure your car. Rates, degree of coverage and services vary, so it pays to shop around and compare. Some recommend paying extra for onsite insurance representation, as it may decrease the likelihood of getting stuck with an unfavourable fault assessment in the case of an accident. Providing a copy of your last vehicle insurance from your home country can sometimes get you a discount if you have a clean driving record.

Taxis

Taxis are also a relatively cheap and convenient way to get around Korean cities, and come in several types. The cheapest are regular *gae-in* taxis, the brightly-coloured four-door sedans that are abundant and can be hailed on any major street. They charge a basic fare of 2,400 won in Seoul (and similar fares in other cities), with the meter tacking on another 100 won at intervals based on distance travelled or time elapsed when traffic is slow. Note that there is a slight fare increase between the hours of midnight and 4am. To hail one, look for a cab that has his red *bincha* light on (signalling vacancy) and raise your hand.

K'ol taeksi (call taxis) can be hailed in the street or by phone through a dispatcher in more out-of-the-way places and cost the same as regular taxis. There are several companies that provide them and all have phone numbers that are so simple that dialling the same digit seven times has about coin-flip odds of connecting you with a dispatcher. The company will send you a text with the dispatched car's number plate; and the driver will ask you for the last four digits of your phone number, to eliminate the chance of someone else grabbing your cab.

Mobeom taeksi (deluxe taxis) are more expensive than *gae-in* taxis and are helmed by better drivers (who must be accident-free for ten years to qualify), though the cars are roughly the same size. *Mobeom* taxis are easily identified by their black colour, and the sometimes over-eager drivers who cajole you upon exiting the train station or airport in the hope that either you won't know that there is a significant difference in price or care.

Jumbo taxis are also available and may be flagged down or booked by phone. These cost the same as regular taxis and are helpful for big groups or for hauling your stuff home after your monthly trip to Costco.

Seoul has also recently instituted an "international taxi" service for foreign guests, which cost slightly more and provide drivers proficient in English, Japanese or Chinese. These can be booked online at www.intltaxi.co.kr or by phone, or may be flagged down at transport hubs like Seoul Station or Incheon International airport.

Tips on taking taxis

There is no tipping generally in Korea, though in the case of taxis, a couple of small exceptions may be made. Even among Koreans, it's common to round up fares to the nearest thousand won. You will also find that drivers often round the fare down when the fare is 100 or 200 won over the last thousand, so it tends to even out over time. A small tip of 1,000 or 2,000 won for drivers who help load and unload heavy bags is also fairly common and never unappreciated.

The majority of taxi drivers will not speak English to any meaningful degree, but you don't really need to speak much Korean to take a cab successfully. Directions are given usually by naming the building or complex to which you are heading, or a nearby landmark, and adding "*-ga chuseyo*" ("please go to"). Korean taxis are all equipped with GPS navigation systems, so having an address handy is a good way to get to places that are harder to explain. Smartphone map applications have also taken a lot of the guesswork and pantomime out of cab rides. And if all else fails, get a Korean friend or colleague on the phone to assist with directions.

In my experience, padding the meter by taking a roundabout route is rare (my baseline of comparison is my hometown, New York), so if you do have some kind of problem (e.g. the driver takes you to the wrong place), it's better to initially give the driver the benefit of the doubt and grant that there may have been some kind of communication problem. If a cabbie is unsure of where your destination is, they will often ask, but it also happens that they will not let on if they don't know where it is, and will either wing it, ask someone else, or find it some other way. You may end up paying a bit more, though it also often happens that a driver knocks a buck or two off the fare to compensate for such a mistake. It may be easier said than done, especially when you're in a hurry to get somewhere, but in those problem cases, try to keep cool, if not for yourself, for the next foreigner he sees on the street. One negative encounter is sometimes all it takes to form a lasting impression.

Sometimes a driver will pass you by because he'd rather not deal with a foreign customer, but often it's because they are nearing the end of their shift or are breaking for a meal (you will sometimes see them signal as if they are eating). If a vacant cab passes you for no apparent reason, sit tight; another one will be along soon.

Korean cab drivers are generally a gregarious lot, and will often pepper you with the usual questions. This is a good opportunity to practice your Korean.

Substitute Drivers

An alternative to driving or taking a taxi is to use a *daeri unjeon* ("substitute driver") service for nights when you have your car but have had one too many drinks to drive home. For a bit more than the cost of a taxi, a driver will drive you home in your own car, and save you the trouble of coming to collect it the next day (and

One last thing: Always wear a seat belt.

remembering where you parked it). To get a driver, simply ask the restaurant/bar manager or parking lot attendant to call one for you.

Public Transportation

South Korea generally has an inexpensive and reliable system of public transportation, and many urban commuters find it to be a relatively cheap, quick and hassle-free way to get from A to B.

For getting around the city, nothing beats the subway for ease, price and speed, especially at rush hour, when traffic slows to a standstill. At this writing, six Korean cities (Seoul, Incheon, Busan, Daejeon, Daegu and Gwangju) have subway systems (called "metro"), and there seem to be new lines under construction all the time.

Seoul's metro system is the most extensive and is fairly easy to navigate. Signs feature English and/or Romanised spellings of Korean place-names, staff are generally helpful, stops are announced in English (as well as Japanese and Chinese), and fares are reasonable. Though they get crowded at peak times, this is often the quickest and least stressful way to cover a lot of distance in the city in the shortest time.

Riders can buy single tickets from vending machines located in every station near the turnstiles. Those who plan to stay awhile can pay with a rechargeable T-Money Card, which are available at subway stations and convenience stores. The cards cost 3,000 won to buy, can be recharged as often as you like at any place which sells them, and save you 100 won per trip. Another option is to pay your bus and subway fares anywhere in Korea by swiping a major Korean credit card at the turnstile.

Six of Korea's major cities have subway systems, with Seoul's the most extensive.

Depending on traffic, city buses are also a good option, as they too are cheap and cover most of the city. You can transfer from bus to subway by swiping your card at the reader near the bus exit.

BANKING

Most medium-to-large bank branches these days seem to have competent English speakers on hand to guide you through your transaction and answer questions. The big national banks (Kookmin, KEB Hana Bank, Shinhan Bank) also have good websites with information in English and other languages, and provide a range of expat-friendly services.

Note that one always boards a Korean bus at the front, and exits from the door in the bus's midsection.

The policies of banks differ, but

in general, foreign residents can open a bank account fairly easily. Go to the bank in person, and bring your Alien Registration Card and your passport, and fill out an application. If your ARC card is still being processed, a passport may suffice—just ask.

FATCA

US citizens and green card holders need to take note of some additional wrinkles regarding overseas banking. In 2010, The Foreign Account Tax Compliance Act (FATCA) passed into law, and it requires Americans who are opening bank accounts overseas to report their bank or investment accounts with the United States Treasury Department if the sum of all accounts exceeds the equivalent of 10,000 dollars. Because the law is new and has already been subject to many revisions, it is recommended to stay up to date with current requirements at the www.irs.gov website, or to consult a tax preparer that specialises in expat services to make sure you are compliant.

At this writing, regular savings accounts pay very little interest. To earn a bit more, you can open a term deposit account, if you don't need to use the funds right away. Debit card accounts are also available. Most banks now also offer online and mobile banking services. Ask about this at the time of opening your account to make these services available.

If you plan to use your ATM card outside of Korea, you should request for that to be made possible at the time you open your account. At some banks, the default ATM card will only work in Korea. If you already have a card and are not sure, it's better to ask at your bank before travelling overseas.

Foreign residents are permitted to send up to US$50,000 a year overseas, to a bank that you designate as the receiver of your funds.

HEALTH CARE AND INSURANCE

South Korea's health care system scores high marks among foreigners who live there, and with many others who visit specifically for treatment. A visit to one of Korea's general hospitals is fairly quick, inexpensive and hassle-free, and the quality of care ranges from satisfactory to superb. In addition to hospitals, there are many smaller private clinics that specialise in different branches of Western medicine, as well as *haneuiwon* (oriental medical clinics) where one can receive traditional treatments like acupuncture, moxibustion or courses of herbal medicine.

Most doctors speak some degree of English, and some speak it quite well. Even doctors with a lower level of general English proficiency will have a large vocabulary of English medical terminology, which is of course quite helpful, even if they occasionally send me running to the dictionary to look up words like nephrolithiasis. There are also several hospitals in Seoul that specialise in treating foreign patients, like Severance Yonsei University Hospital, Asan Medical Center, Samsung Chaeil Hospital and the Seoul Foreign Clinic, all of which have speakers of several languages on hand to assist you.

Medical Tourism

For the past decade or so, the Korean government has been actively promoting South Korea as a "medical tourism" destination, and tens of thousands of people from China, Japan, the US and elsewhere have been drawn to Korea to take advantage of its low-cost, high-quality health care, undergoing treatments and procedures ranging from a triple bypass to a tummy tuck, often at a fraction of the cost of comparable procedures in their home countries. Many newer facilities combine hospitals with hotel-style accommodation and other amenities, and changes in the law have made it easier for patients to acquire longer-term visas more easily. A lengthy hospital stay may not be what leaps to mind as most people's idea of a dream vacation, but for many who are facing expensive health care bills or lengthy waiting periods for treatment, a trip to Korea may be just what the doctor ordered.

Insurance

South Korea has a system of national health insurance in which all citizens and documented foreign nationals are enrolled, and which covers non-elective medical treatments. Those who are working pay half of their NHI deductible, while their employer pays the remainder. If you are admitted to a hospital or clinic, you will be responsible for a co-payment of around 20%, while outpatient treatments may be slightly higher, but still quite inexpensive. By way of example, a recent visit to a local clinic, where I was examined by a physician and prescribed a course of antibiotics for a throat infection, set me back about 15,000 won (USD$13.00), drugs included. If you have questions about the national health insurance, contact the National Health Insurance Corporation at their English helpline (02-390-2000) or visit their branch office nearest you.

While most foreign residents find the NHI to be sufficient, some get private insurance on top of that for extra peace of mind in the case of a catastrophic injury or illness that requires lengthy hospitalisation or repatriation. People working on one-year contracts should be aware that a health problem that renders you unable to work for several weeks can result in the legal termination of a work contract and thus the loss of your national insurance. Such cases are rare, but they do happen, so give some thought to which approach works best for you. Also note that if you travel abroad during your Korea sojourn, you should consider getting travel insurance, as the Korean NHI does not cover you outside of Korea.

Other Health Services

Because of the generally high quality and relatively low cost of medical care in Korea, many people opt to have elective procedures done here. Some of the other common health services in Korea you may consider taking advantage of are:

Cosmetic Surgery

With twenty people in a thousand electing to undergo some form of cosmetic procedure, South Korea has the world's highest per capita rate of cosmetic surgery (the United States is a distant second at 13 per 1,000), a stat that has earned Korea the nickname of "Plastic Surgery Capital of the World". V-shaped jawlines, rhinoplasty, liposuction and double eyelids top the list of popular procedures, as tens of thousands of Koreans each year go under the knife to alter their appearance. While some decry it as a needless and risky form of vanity, to many others, plastic surgery gives a boost to self-confidence, positively affects their work and marriage prospects, and is seen as a commonplace accoutrement in an increasingly competitive society.

Dentistry

High quality dentistry is very affordable in Korea, and many dentists who speak English advertise online and in English print media. Many of them are trained in the US and Canada and will have their credentials displayed proudly and prominently in their reception areas. If you've been putting off that root canal or crown replacement, Korea is a good place to have it sorted out.

Health and Safety Tips and Info

Since the early 1990s, the rapidly increasing number of motor vehicles on Korea's roads has resulted in an equally rapid increase in traffic accidents. Recent initiatives like seat belt laws, speed trap cameras, drunk-driving crackdowns and lowered speed limits have had a positive effect, but South Korea still sits well above the OECD average for road accidents and traffic fatalities. Be extra vigilant on the roads, especially as a pedestrian. In particular, keep an eye out for motorbike drivers, who are more likely to turn up in places you may not expect, like sidewalks, the gaps between cars, hugging the curb or on the wrong side of the road.

Tap water is fine for brushing your teeth and is reported to be safe to drink, though most people seem to prefer bottled or filtered water.

Koreans often wear surgical masks when they are sick to help stem the transmission of airborne pathogens during cold and flu season. Pharmacies sell a variety of inexpensive masks; some even bear designs to make them more appealing to kids and fashion-conscious flu sufferers.

No vaccinations are required to enter Korea. If you intend to stay for a long time, you may want to get your vaccinations up to date (e.g. Hepatitis A and B, polio, measles, rubella, tetanus, etc), but if you don't, you can easily get caught up at any major hospital. In Korea's densely populated cities, colds and flu seemingly hit everyone at once in the winter. Getting an annual flu shot at a local clinic won't hurt for more than a second, and will earn you resistance and a lolly for your courage.

Spring can be tough on people who suffer from pollen allergies. A visit to an ENT specialist or a pharmacy can get you set up with medicines to treat your symptoms. Many Koreans don masks during peak pollen season, and also during days that are particularly smoggy or have high concentrations of airborne dust.

WOMEN'S SAFETY

In eighteen years in Korea I have yet to find a street I would be afraid to walk down, day or night, or encounter a situation where I felt threatened, and all of my male friends echo the same sentiments. Women generally say they feel safe too, but they are always quick to add a few caveats and words of caution. The following is a distillation of several years of experience from female friends and acquaintances.

Many of the same general rules for city living apply in Korea. Avoid walking home alone at night, particularly if you live on a darker street with few or no people around, and be aware of your surroundings. In practice, this can mean not wearing earphones when walking around, being mindful of your glass in a club or bar and not accepting a drink that you have not seen poured from someone you don't know. Above all, guard against complacency.

Because Korea is generally safe, many people drop their guard, and become vulnerable to an assault, which are rare but not unheard of.

In a similar vein, don't be lulled by CCTV cameras. There is hardly a patch of land anywhere in Seoul that is not within the sweep of a CCTV camera, and most lobbies, stairwells, streets and stores now have cameras protruding from seemingly every corner, post and ceiling. From this writer's perspective, though the presence of a camera probably does deter some crime, CCTV tends to be more valuable as photographic evidence *after* a crime has already occurred. In short, the cameras may help, but it shouldn't be relied on as a shield.

When taking a taxi alone at night, many women report conspicuously taking a picture of the car's number plate or the driver's taxi license (posted on the glove compartment) and sending it to a friend on entering the taxi, to thwart a would-be offender.

Check in with friends after parting for the night. Ask friends to call or text when they arrive, and let them know when you arrive safely. Conspicuously messaging or calling someone from the car may decrease the likelihood of an assault.

If you do have a problem, call the police. There are

mixed opinions of Korean police among the foreign community, especially as regards cases involving a sexual assault. In some cases, victims report that police have been slow or reluctant to respond, have downplayed the seriousness of their complaint or have partly blamed them for their misfortune. However, in other cases, they do their jobs competently and professionally; and in cases in which a foreign woman has been attacked, they have sometimes gone far above and beyond the call, as was the case with an acquaintance of mine, who was stalked to her door and fought off a would-be assailant. Local police responded by beefing up patrols in her neighbourhood, offering to walk her home from the subway every day and vigorously investigating the attack. While not every report will be handled in this way, one can't merely assume that reporting a crime is futile either. "Never feel like you can't call the police," she advises, as it's the only way of possibly preventing the same thing from happening to someone else.

To call the police in an emergency or to report a crime, dial 112 from any phone. An English translator will be made available to you if you ask.

GETTING A PHONE

There are many options for getting a phone set up in Korea, and they differ according to the type of phone or plan you want, for what length of time, as well as your status in the country.

Short term phone rentals are available at airports and tend to offer reasonable rates for short term stays. Service desks can be found easily around any airport with international connections.

For longer stays (a few months to a year), prepaid mobile phones are generally the quickest and easiest to get set up. The rates per minute are higher than regular monthly plans, but you can buy a used phone very cheaply (under 20,000 won) as opposed to shelling out several hundreds of thousands of won for a new one. If you intend to use data (Internet) however, a phone plan may be the way to go, as prepaid options either don't include data or charge exorbitant rates.

For longer stays, monthly plans can be better, but will vary in availability depending on the length of your stay in Korea. For stays of less than two years, this may not be an option, as purchasing a phone in Korea at this writing requires a two-year contract, but some foreigners who stay less than two years report signing up anyway and paying off the phone when they leave. If you do so, expect to pay a deposit, as past experience has made phone companies justifiably wary of foreigners skipping out on unpaid phone contracts.

Korea has three main carriers through which to subscribe to mobile networks: SK Telecom, Olleh and LG U+. Olleh and SK Telecom tend to be most highly recommended and are comparable in terms of price and service. Phone shops are easy to find in any commercial district. To get a phone you will have to bring your passport, alien registration card and your bank account information or Korean credit card. Bringing a Korean-speaking friend can also be a help in making sure you understand the terms of the contract.

You can bring your own phone to Korea, but it must be unlocked, and support the 2.1 GHz 3G WCDMA network, which is true of most new phones these days, but it's still good to check. Smartphones will also work, and the newer models (iPhone 5 or later, or Samsung Galaxy Note or S) tend to be more hassle-free. If you're not sure if your phone is unlocked or meets these requirements, contacting your provider can sort it out. Some recommend bringing a phone because it admits non-contract service options that allow you to pay month by month, and cancel a month in advance when you leave Korea. To buy a SIM card, head to one of the bigger phone shops.

If having a functional phone upon arrival is imperative, and you're not up for sorting it yourself, you can use a service like The Arrival Store (www.thearrivalstore.com), who can have a phone waiting for you at the airport and don't require a Korean ID. Many people have found this service useful because an ARC card can take weeks to process, and you will be either phoneless or using a cheap rental until you have the ARC card in hand.

KOREA'S INTERNET SPEED
IS THE FASTEST IN THE WORLD
KOREA'S KIDS ARE THE
HAPPIEST!

INTERNET

At 29 mbps, Korea's average Internet speed is the fastest in the world, clocking in at over four times the global average and making visitors to Korea more wont to complain about the "slow" connection speeds during visits back to their home countries.

Korea has a few Internet service providers, who offer various types of connections and lengths of contract. Korea Telecom (KT) is the biggest provider of broadband DSL (Megapass) and hot spot access (Nespot). Dial-up connections are available, but Korea's high population density allows for relatively cheap broadband service (around 30,000 won per month), and has made it the more popular option by far.

If you don't use the Internet frequently and don't need it at home, note that most coffee shops these days provide free wifi to customers, and generally let you stay as long as you want. Visiting a PC bang is another alternative to a home hookup. PC bangs are very common and offer cheap hourly rates (between one and two thousand won per hour), and are often fitted out with large monitors, powerful PCs, and the fastest Internet connections you're likely to find anywhere. For Internet browsing, e-mail, gaming etc, these are a good

A university district PC bang on a typical afternoon.

option, but if you're looking to get some work done, note that PC bangs can be quite loud, as the majority of customers are playing games (and trash-talking their friends who are often sitting nearby).

CABLE TV

Satellite or cable TV is available throughout the peninsula, and can be installed by different providers. Price varies according to company, region, package, etc.

Phone Etiquette

Around the world, etiquette is forever playing catch-up to technological advance and social change, and Korea is no exception. "Phone etiquette" indeed often seems like an oxymoron, as people speak loudly in public places, stare at their phones in the company of friends and play games with annoying sound effects full volume. As in the rest of the world, the situation is improving over time, and the same sort of general rules appear to be emerging:

- Use earphones when listening to music or watching a video in a public place.

- If you must take a call while out with someone, it's acceptable to excuse yourself to go answer it. Non-essential calls and texts can wait.

- If you have to take a call in a crowded place (like a subway, bus, office, etc), lower your voice.

Satellite costs more to install (in the neighbourhood of 600,000 won) but offers a wider range of channels, including foreign language channels. Cable is somewhat cheaper to set up, though it has less English-language programming. One upside of cable is that your cable package can usually be bundled with an Internet installation package as well, killing two birds with one stone.

GETTING A VISA

Because Korea participates in reciprocal visa waiver agreements, citizens of most countries may enter Korea for

90 days without a visa (Canadian citizens get six months). If you intend to stay for longer than 90 days, or will be studying or working in Korea in some capacity, you will need to apply for the visa appropriate to your intended sojourn at a Korean embassy or consular office prior to arrival.

If you intend to do your job-seeking in Korea, upon securing an offer of employment, you will have to leave Korea to apply for your visa. Most people do their visa run to Fukuoka, Japan, which is easily reached by air or by ferry from Busan in less than three hours. Submitting your application and relevant documents before 11:00am at the Korean consulate will ensure you have your visa waiting for you the following morning. It's always good to double-check that you have the required documents before leaving.

The range of visa types and requirements is too great to describe here in detail; to check your eligibility for various visa types (business, education, student, entertainment, investor, etc), as well as the relevant procedure for applying and documents required, go to www.hikorea.go.kr.

FOREIGN AND INTERNATIONAL SCHOOLS

Foreign and international schools share broad similarities but differ in their student populations. As the name suggests, foreign schools are primarily for foreign students, though they may reserve space for a limited number of Korean students. International schools have more flexibility in admitting Koreans, and are popular both with foreign families and with Koreans who wish to prepare their children for higher education overseas.

Admission requirements and application processes vary,

but students will have to show a passport, school transcripts, birth certificate and standardised test scores (where applicable). Many schools also administer an entrance exam and require interviews of prospective students. Depending on the school, there may be a waiting list, and tuition can range from 10 to 25 million won per year.

Seoul
Pre-schools
British International Kindergarten – www.britishschool.co.kr

Namsan International Kindergarten – Operated by the Seoul Foreign School (see below).

Early Childhood Learning Center – Offers programs for children ages 2 through 6 (kindergarten), guided by the International Primary Curriculum (IPC). www.eclcseoul.com

Primary and Secondary Schools
Seoul Foreign School – Founded in 1912, Seoul Foreign School is the oldest foreign school in Korea. SFS offers either a K-12 American curriculum or the English National curriculum, culminating in an International Baccalaureate (IB) diploma. www.seoulforeign.org

Korea International School – US K-12 curriculum. Has two Seoul campuses and a third in Jejudo. www.kis.kr

Seoul International School – US K-12 curriculum. www.siskorea.org

Yongsan International School of Seoul – A Christian school close to the international communities of Yongsan (near Yongsan Garrison). www.yisseoul.org

Asia Pacific International School – Christian school with a WASC-accredited K-12 programme. www.apis.org

Dwight School Seoul – accredited with the Council of International Schools (CIS), and leads to an International Baccalaureate (IB) diploma. www.dwight.or.kr

EtonHouse Prep – Based on the British preparatory education system for students aged 2 to 13, and is affiliated with EtonHouse International Education Group. www.prep.etonhousekorea.com

Dulwich College School – Follows the English National curriculum, the International GSCE syllabus, and the International Baccalaureate Diploma Programme. www.dulwich-seoul.kr

Other Cities

The greatest concentration of foreign schools is in Seoul, but other foreign and international schools can be found in cities throughout the country.

Chadwick International – a sister school of Chadwick School in Palos Verdes, California. Located in the Songdo International District in Incheon. www.chadwickinternational.org

Taejeon Christian International School (Daejeon) – Founded by American Christian missionaries in 1958, they offer K-12 programs leading to an IB diploma.

Busan Foreign School – Partnered with Seoul Foreign School and enjoys an excellent reputation for preparing students for higher education overseas. US curriculum. www.busanforeignschool.org

Busan International Foreign School – Pre-k through 12th grade, leading to an IB diploma. www.bifskorea.org

Daegu International School – US curriculum, grades K-12. www.dis.sc.kr

Kwangju Foreign School (Gwangju) – Pre-K through 12, American curriculum, WASC accredited.

South Korea also has foreign schools where languages other than English or Korean are the primary languages of instruction. The following are some of the schools in the Seoul area; check online for schools outside the capital region.

Deutsche Schule Seoul – dsseoul.org

Lycee Francaise de Seoul – lfseoul.org

The Japanese School in Seoul – Programmes from kindergarten through middle school. www.sjs.or.kr

Chinese Primary School – www.hanxiao.or.kr

CHAPTER 6

FOOD AND DRINK

> **❝** The average Korean does not eat that he may live, but lives that he may eat. **❞**

— Percival Lowell

When I first came to Korea, I knew nothing at all about Korean food, and the longer I stayed, the more I wondered why that was the case. Unlike the popular cuisines of their neighbours the Chinese and the Japanese, Korean food is relatively less known, but boasts such a remarkable variety of dishes and regional variations that it now seems I could spend my life here and not have sampled everything.

If Korean food is underrated internationally, it is not underrated by the locals; few people are more frankly enamoured of their national cuisine than the Koreans. And rightly so: Korean food is one of the things that most foreigners fall in love with soon after arrival, and is one of the things they find themselves missing when they leave, a common refrain that is humorously encapsulated in an old story from the Korean War that tells of an American POW, who upon his reunion with his family, told his wife that she simply had to learn how to make kimchi.

Korean food may not enjoy the popularity of Japanese and Chinese, but that is changing as word slowly gets out. The *Hallyu* (Korean Wave) phenomenon has steadily raised awareness of Korean culture to people across Asia, Europe and North America, while second-generation Korean-American restaurateurs in cities like New York and Los Angeles are making the tastes of their elders available to a public that is increasingly keen for new experiences and aware of the health benefits of fermented "slow foods" like kimchi. Korean food has also caught the attention of many high-profile Western commentators, like writer and chef Anthony Bourdain, who visited Korea in the winter of 2014 to shoot an episode on Korean food for CNN's *Parts Unknown*. The trip apparently made quite an impression on Bourdain, because he was still raving about it a year later, calling Korean cuisine a "bottomless bringer of culture" and the thing that "everybody wants and is craving… spicy, funky, fermented, that whole spectrum of flavours."

Many visitors to Korea are surprised at the richness and variety of the Korean menu, from marinated meats sizzling over charcoal to robust soups to savour slowly. Because Korean cooking tends to centre on a few key condiments and sauces, the variety is not so much to be found in the ranges of flavouring agents available (as compared to the flavour palette of say, French, Indian or Thai), but in the vast range of ingredients and combinations it employs. Meats, roots, greens, fruits, grains and shoots turn up on the Korean table in delightful combinations.

Eating Korean is also an exercise in culture, not so much because of what they eat, but how. Meals are almost always a shared experience that bring friends and families together, create and maintain bonds between staff, management and organisation, and often serve as the launching pad and recurring theme of a night on the town. Various dishes are imbued with significance that goes far beyond their nutritional content, and many are tied to holidays, superstition, medicinal practice, folklore, tradition and ritual. To focus solely on the flavours is to miss half the story.

Entire books are written on Korean food, but the following chapter is a sampling of some of the more common dishes you will encounter, and others not so common that you should consider encountering as soon as possible.

THE BUILDING BLOCKS
Gochu

Gochu (Korean chilli pepper) appears in many forms, and is what gives many Korean dishes its reddish colour and spicy flavour. *Gochugaru* (dried pepper flakes) is used as a seasoning in many dishes, most famously in kimchi, or to create a condiment called *gochujang*, a spicy-sweet paste made from *gochugaru*, soybean paste, rice flour and malt. *Gochujang* is fermented in earthenware jars called *onggi* (or more often sold in plastic tubs at the local supermarket), and is used to flavour a variety of dishes like *dakkalbi*, *ddeokbokki*, *bibimbap* and *nakjibokkeum*. Fresh, green chilli peppers also turn up on the table as a common side dish with Korean barbecue, and can range from mild to murderous. Depending on your pain threshold, you may want to ask your server before indulging.

Soy Beans
The soybean is another foundational element upon which many Korean dishes are built. Soybeans are boiled, mashed

and dried, and the resulting mass (called *meju*) is fermented in brine to make soy sauce, which is used as both a condiment and ingredient in dishes too numerous to name. The leftover *meju* is processed into a deep, tangy paste called *doenjang*, a sharper, bare-knuckled cousin of Japanese miso, which powers everything from soup stocks to the dipping condiments for grilled meats.

Onggi

Rice

Though many grains may appear on the Korean table, the most common hands-down is *bap* (short-grain glutinous rice). As in many Asian cultures, rice is a feature of most meals in Korea, either as an accompaniment to a main dish, as the base of a stir-fry or *bibimbap*, or as a basic, get-out-the-door breakfast with a few pieces of kimchi. Rice is so central to the Korean food universe that it is virtually synonymous with food itself. When a Korean asks you, "*Bap meogeosseoyo*?" he is literally asking you, "Have you eaten rice?", but one answers in the affirmative whether one has eaten *bibimbap* or a Big Mac.

Kimchi

Baechu Kimchi—that pungent, red-tinged cabbage with the fiery kick—so often appears as a side dish and cooking ingredient that it is the food most closely associated with Korea itself. Koreans have been making various types of kimchi since at least the Three Kingdoms period (though in different, pepper-less, forms), and possibly much longer than that. However long it has been around, kimchi today is much more than a food—it's a cultural touchstone to millions of Koreans and a virtually inseparable component of their cultural identity. It's the food that my Korean friends are most likely to report craving when they move overseas, and the one they are most likely to pack in their suitcases when they travel, as my wife has done on every overseas trip except to New York, but only after I assured her we would be able to find plenty of kimchi there.

Traditionally, Koreans have made kimchi in the late fall, during the kimchi-making season known as *kimjang*. Today, kimchi is available for purchase year-round, and while many households still make their own supply, the *kimjang* tradition appears to be on the wane among younger generations, who often lack the time, inclination or know-how to make it themselves.

Among the households who still craft their own, *kimjang* is often a cooperative affair, bringing together friends, neighbours and several generations of family to lighten the work and divvy up the product. To make *baechu kimchi* ("cabbage kimchi"), several heads of cabbage are first salted and rinsed. Soon after, they are seasoned with red pepper, garlic and either brine shrimp or an anchovy sauce called *jeotgal*, and then left to ferment for anywhere from a week to a year or more. Fresh kimchi can be eaten immediately, and is usually sampled the same day along with some *bossam* (steamed pork), but like blue jeans, fine wine and Dame Judi Dench, kimchi tends to get better with age. If a Korean friend offers you some of her mom's two-year old kimchi, she is not unloading on you; she's inviting you to partake in a special treat.

Kimchi in Space

When Korea's first astronaut, bio-engineer Yi So-yeon, blasted off in 2008 for the International Space Station, she carried with her a good supply of kimchi. Prior to the flight, the kimchi had to be irradiated to kill off any bacteria that might hitch along for the ride to space. According to Yi, the irradiation process made the kimchi come out looking a bit worse for wear. "I cannot say it's a really tasteful kimchi," she reported, "but I still like it because I can feel my home."

In the past, once the kimchi was made, it was stored underground in earthenware jars, which kept it cool in the summer and prevented it from freezing in winter. Some older folks with outdoor space still store it in this way, but because most people today live in apartments, kimchi is more often refrigerated, usually in a separate *kimchi naengjanggo* (kimchi refrigerator) to keep its pungent aroma from permeating every other thing in the fridge and its immediate vicinity.

Koreans have long touted kimchi as a medicinal food, and at various times have proclaimed it to be a remedy for anything from the common cold to cancer. Science today tells us that kimchi is a bona fide "superfood" with many proven health benefits: rich in minerals and vitamins A and C, fibre to promote colon health, lactobacilli that aid digestion and spices to boost metabolism. When eaten daily in moderate quantities, kimchi has many beneficial effects, though some doctors warn that because of kimchi's high salt content, one should be wary of overdoing it.

Though kimchi is most often associated with *baechu kimchi* (cabbage kimchi), it actually refers to an entire class of fermented vegetables comprising over 200 types and regional variations. Some of the other common types of kimchi are:

Mul kimchi or "water kimchi" refers to various types of kimchi served in cool brine. They can be made from various ingredients (radish, cabbage, pear, cucumber), and generally lack the red pepper of their spicier namesakes. A good place to start for first-timers.

Baek kimchi, or "white kimchi" is cabbage kimchi minus the red pepper, and is what kimchi used to look like prior to the introduction of the chilli pepper to Korea sometime during the Joseon Dynasty.

Chonggak kimchi is made from long slices of young radish with the greens still attached, which is said to resemble the top-knot hairstyle common among *chonggak* (bachelors) during the Joseon Dynasty.

Ggakdugi is radish kimchi that is cut into cubes. "*Ggakdugi*" is also used as a slang word for "gangster", as the squarish shape of the radish resembles the flat-top haircuts often sported by Korean wise guys.

BANCHAN

The Korean table can have anywhere from one to several dozen side dishes, or *banchan*. These are provided at no extra cost, and are considered an important component to every meal to complement and round it out. Korean diners take *banchan* seriously, and often the choice of a favourite restaurant will come down the quality and quantity of their *banchan*. You are not expected (nor advised) to attempt to finish them all, but do try to at least sample each. If you do plow through them, the staff will also refill them at no charge.

Even simple meals may come with a variety of *banchan* for diners to share.

Banchan can vary widely from restaurant to restaurant and region to region. *Baechu kimchi* is usually a given, but you may also find *oi kimchi* (cucumber kimchi), *ggakdugi* (cubed radish kimchi), *dongchimi* (water radish kimchi), or some other variety. Other common *banchan* are: *sigeumchi muchim* (soy and sesame spinach), *kongnameul muchim* (seasoned bean sprouts) *maneul jangajji* (pickled garlic cloves), *gyeran jjim* (steamed eggs), raw green chilli peppers with dip, *gaji nameul* (soy-marinated eggplant), *myeolchi bokkeum* (honey glazed, stir-fried anchovies), *ojingeochae bokkeum* (dried squid with gochujang dip), *jeon* (savory pancakes), *dubu jorim* (braised tofu) and *japchae* (stir-fried glass noodles).

MEAT DISHES

Koreans do meat in several ways, but the most popular and iconic are the various types of Korean barbecue. Grilled meats are cooked at the centre of the table, either by a harried server, or more often by your own party, adding a fun DIY element to the meal. Whether it's beef, pork or fowl, grilled meats are often bundled up in a leaf (usually lettuce or perilla) and topped with other seasonings and condiments (marinated onions, garlic, *samjang*, etc), though some prefer to merely dip the meat and pop it in their mouths. There are no fixed rules; experiment and see what you like.

Chimaek

Food trends come and go, but one of the most stable trends of the past few years is *chimaek*, or, the pairing of fried chicken with beer, which is reflected in the name: "chi" from chicken and "*maek*" from maekju (beer). Koreans have been consuming chicken and beer together for quite some time, but the pairing became an official "thing" in 2014, when the heroine of the popular drama *My Love from the Star* professed her love of the dish as just the thing for a snowy day. Since then, the demand for chicken and beer combos has risen in Korea, as well as in neighbouring China, where the show was very popular and was credited by the Chinese government in almost single-handedly reviving the sagging poultry industry after an outbreak of avian influenza in 2013.

Though purists may disagree over what constitutes *chimaek*, the particular style of the chicken, as well as the beer it is paired with, can vary widely, from crispy battered wings to whole roasted chickens in a garlicky-soy sauce. Whatever you decide on, the good news is you are never far from a chicken place; Korea now boasts upwards of 20,000 chicken restaurants that will deliver chicken—and often beer—to your door. Yes, please, and *thank you*.

A delivery rider makes his rounds.

Bulgogi

Strips of beef are marinated in a sweetened soy sauce and grilled at the table. The name means "fire meat", not because it's spicy, but because of the cooking method. *Bulgogi* is a can't-miss for all but vegetarians, and was not coincidentally the very first meal I was treated to by my first employer in Korea. The ever-popular *bulgogi* even turns up in tacos, on pizzas and on fast food menus, like McDonald's Bulgogi Burger and Costco's Bulgogi Bake.

Galbi

Galbi means ribs, and by itself usually refers to beef ribs (*sogalbi*) but can also be pork (*dwaeji galbi*). Feel free to use your hands, the better to clean them to the bone.

Dakgalbi

Chicken marinated in a spicy *gochujang* base is probably more deserving of the name "fire meat", but that was already taken. The "*galbi*" is also misleading, as there is no rib meat, but whatever you call it, the result is magic. It can be grilled or stir-fried, usually with diced cabbage, green onion, potatoes and *ddeok*. The *dakgalbi* in Chuncheon, the capital of Gangwon Province, is particularly famous and is worth a stop if you are passing through.

Samgyeopsal

One session with these thick, fatty pieces of pork belly and you will never look at bacon the same way again. *Samgyeopsal* is often paired with *soju*, though beer works just as well.

Steamed Meats

Though barbecue is rightly famous, it isn't the only game in town. Some of the more interesting selection of steamed meat dishes are:

Galbijjim is steamed beef ribs with carrots that melt in your mouth. It was traditionally served on holidays like Seollal and Chuseok, but is now available year round.

Jjimdak is chunks of chicken stewed in a sweet sauce with potatoes, carrots and glass noodles. One of the lesser-known gems of the Korean food universe.

Bossam is pork belly that is boiled (or steamed) and sliced, served with garlic, onion and *samjang*. *Bossam* is traditionally served with the newly-made kimchi during *kimjang*, and also makes a dependable side dish for a serious drinking session.

Seafood

Perhaps nothing better illustrates the variety of the Korean menu than their approach to seafood. There is scarcely an aquatic plant or animal species within a thousand miles of the Korean peninsula that generations of Korean cooks have not long ago figured out what to do with. A trip to a Busan *pojang macha* reveals flora and fauna you never knew existed, never mind tasted amazing.

The Korean word for "fish" (*mulgogi*) is itself indicative of the Korean openness to the sea's bounty: a compound formed of the word for "water" (*mul*) and "meat" (*gogi*), it serves not only to label a common class of animals, but hints at a worldview, a working assumption that every swimming denizen of the sea is game unless proven otherwise.

While seafood plays a supporting role in a wide array of many otherwise non-seafood dishes (e.g. as the base of a soup stock, as a seasoning when fermenting kimchi or as a bit player in roll of *kimbap* or a stir-fry), in the following dishes it's the star of the show.

Hwae is the Korean take on sliced raw fish, better known to Westerners by its Japanese name, *sashimi*. Fish markets around the peninsula boast a wide array of species, but some popular favourites are sea bream, sea bass, mullet, porgy, rockfish, yellowtail and flatfish. Presentation sometimes takes a back seat to speed, but the flavours seldom disappoint, and the freshness is unquestionable.

The tanks in front of *hwae jip* ("raw fish places") can often resemble small aquariums.

Chobap is what Westerners know as sushi: slices of fish or other goodies (beef, egg, shellfish, octopus) perched atop a hand-shaped bed of rice. *Chobap* is relatively inexpensive and is available in many places, from supermarket seafood sections to high-end sushi bars.

San nakji means live octopus, and fans of the 2003 film *Old Boy* never forget the scene in which Daesu (played by Choi Min-sik) eats a large, writhing octopus, head and all. If that put you off your appetite, the good news is that nobody except mysterious characters in noir thrillers eats them that way. To prepare *san nakji*, octopus are sliced up quickly and served with sesame oil, which serves less as a seasoning than as a lubricant to prevent the still-active suckers from getting caught on the way down. It's not everyone's cup of tea, but it always makes a good story for the folks back home.

Haemul pajeon is a style of *jeon* that originated in Busan and is studded with various types of seafood like shrimp, octopus, shellfish or squid. Once you've tried it, it's hard to eat *jeon* any other way.

Jjambbong is a spicy, Korean-Chinese noodle dish that is so loaded with sea critters that digging into a bowl can itself feel like a fishing expedition.

Nakji bokkeum is a dish where baby octopus goes into a pot with some veggies, gochujang and water, and is cooked down to a spicy sweet reduction and tossed with rice and glass noodles. Hurts so good!

Jangeogui means grilled eel. Seasoned freshwater eel is filleted, sliced and tossed on the grill, often before it has a chance to stop moving, and served with *chojang* and veggies to wrap it all up. Jangeogui featured in the first meal my wife ever cooked for me, and thus served as another small indication that I had married well.

An eel fisherman unloads his catch.

Jeonbokjuk is a simple delicacy flavoured with slices of fresh abalone. Koreans do several varieties of *juk* (rice porridge)—pumpkin, bean, pine nut and many others—but the perennial favourite is arguably *jeonbokjuk*. Because it is nutritious and easy to digest, *juk* is often fed to young children and to people recuperating from an illness, though people of all ages enjoy its creamy texture and savoury flavour. Many Koreans consider *jeonbokjuk* a must-eat on any visit to Jejudo, where wild abalone are harvested by Jejudo's famous *haenyeo* (female skin divers), who dive to depths of up to 20 metres to gather them.

SOUPS AND STEWS

To many Koreans, no meal is complete without some form of soup, either as a side dish to accompany a larger meal, or as a main dish in itself with rice and *banchan* on the side. Korean cuisine boasts a great variety of satisfying soups, and they are generally classed into three main categories: *guk*, *tang*, and *jjigae*. *Guk* tends to feature a lighter, more subtle broth and features one or a few ingredients, while the *jjigae* is more flavourful and thick, and straddles the line between soup and stew. A *tang* is a rich soup that requires a longer preparation time and features a deep, flavourful broth.

The following is not nearly an exhaustive list, but is a rundown of the more common soups and stews on the Korean menu.

Deonjangjjiggae is the most common and popular of the *jjigae*. Flavoured with mung bean paste (*doenjang*), it also contains tofu, green onion, and in different regions may be laden with sea squirt, crab, beef, shrimp or other goodies. Not to be missed, as if such a thing were possible.

Kimchijjigae, or kimchi stew, is, along with *doenjangjjigae*, another common classic that is a staple for many people and a common lunch dish or side to a BBQ meal. Beef, pork or seafood goes in a pot with some kimchi, scallions and garlic, which are then boiled in an anchovy stock. The older the kimchi, the better, as this gives it a more complex flavour.

Budaejjigae, or "army base stew", takes its name from its origins during the Korean War, when Mother Necessity inspired Koreans to put black-market Spam and hot dogs into a pot with whatever ingredients were available, thus giving birth to a flavourful fusion of Korean sensibilities and American components. Though there are many variations on the theme, kimchi and *gochujang* form the base, and it may also include baked beans, *ramyeon* noodles, green onions, tofu, beef and slices of American cheese. Sounds funky, I know, but many who try it agree that it is a textbook case of the whole being greater than the sum of the parts.

Samgyetang is a personal favourite: a whole chicken stuffed with rice, chestnut, garlic, ginseng, and jujube, simmered in a succulent broth and garnished with diced green onion. Traditionally, *samgyetang* is a summer dish, though my own extensive experimentation has confirmed that it works equally well year-round, especially during cold season, where it doubles as a potent form of Jewish penicillin.

Gomtang, or oxtail soup, doesn't have many ingredients— oxtail, green onions and salt—and while this may sound like it makes for a boring, bare bones soup, when the broth is done right it hits the spot and warms the coldest bones.

Seolleongtang is a soup made from beef bones and brisket, which are simmered for hours and produce a rich, whitish broth. It is said to have originated by royal edict during the Shilla Dynasty, in an effort to make the most of scarce meat. Mission accomplished.

Galbitang features beef ribs that are boiled until they are melt-in-your-mouth soft. Another hearty beef-based soup.

Gamjatang means "potato soup". It may seem strange that a soup with a name like that should only sometimes actually include potatoes, but the other ingredients more than make up for it: pork on the bone, *doenjang*, *gochujang*, cabbage, mushrooms, soybean sprouts and perilla leaves make for a hearty meal and robust flavour.

Maeuntang is a soup of large chunks of fish (usually snapper, cod or sea bass) with mushrooms, *ssukgat* (garland chrysanthemum) and onions. The name means "spicy soup", thanks to the *gochujang* and *gochugaru* that power the broth.

Haejangguk is a popular hangover remedy, and for this reason, many places that serve it stay open all night and get busy in the wee hours, as late night revellers come in for a bowl to try to avoid paying the piper his full due. Haejangguk is flavoured with doenjang and contains congealed ox blood cut into chunks, with a liberal smattering of bean sprouts and other veggies to round it out. If the blood of an ox doesn't put you back on your feet, I don't know what will.

Ddeokguk features *ddeok* (rice cake) sliced into coin-shaped pieces and tossed in a meaty broth, then garnished with a boiled egg and crumbled *kim* (dried seaweed). Eating *ddeokguk* on Lunar New Year ensures that you age one year along with the rest of Korea; or just eat it anytime because it's good.

Miyeokguk is a simple soup made with beef and a dark-green edible seaweed called *miyeok*. Koreans enjoy it year-round, but it has special significance as a traditional birthday breakfast, and as a food commonly given to breastfeeding mothers because of its high calcium content. Just don't give it to a student who is taking a test that day—according to superstition, the slippery texture of the seaweed may cause the correct answers to "slip" away from you.

Kongnamulguk is a light, simple, refreshing soup of bean sprouts and scallions in an anchovy broth, sometimes seasoned with red pepper flakes for a little zing. Easy to prepare, this is a common go-to soup for Koreans at home, and is great for nursing a cold or a hangover.

Dwaejigukbap ("pork rice soup") is a hearty soup made from tender cuts of pork, onions and rice, which diners season to taste with *gochujang*, garlic chives and brine shrimp. *Sundaegukbap* is a variation that adds *sundae* (Korean-style blood sausage) either in lieu of or in addition to the pork. *Dwaejigukbap* is a signature dish of South Gyoungsang Province, and in particular Busan, whose version of this blue-collar classic many Koreans (and this author) consider to be the gold standard.

NOODLES

Korean noodles come in a variety of shapes, lengths, compositions and cooking styles. Some dishes can be a simple snack or meal in themselves; sometimes they are served as a side dish or as a substitute for rice.

Naengmyeon is a popular summer dish of thin buckwheat noodles served cold, flavoured with vinegar, mustard, cucumber and a boiled egg. There is also a spicy variety called *bibim naengmyeon*.

Japchae is a dish of glass noodles tossed with beef and veggies, served hot or cold, usually as a side dish.

Jajjangmyeon is a Chinese-Korean fusion dish of noodles in a black bean sauce.

Ramyeon are instant noodles that originated in Japan as a cheap quick alternative to *ramen*, but have embedded themselves deeply in Korea, where they have their own spin and are sold in several flavours, and are popular with Koreans of all ages.

Kalguksu are wheat flour noodles in an anchovy broth with scallions and other ingredients, making for a cheap and delicious pick-me-up on shopping excursions in the old markets.

Kalguksu

STREET FOOD

Street food carts can be found all over Korea—in traditional markets, school and university districts and heavily trafficked downtown shopping areas—selling a variety of quick bites to fuel a shopping spree, stroll or just tide you over until dinnertime. Street food is very popular in Korea; even modern supermarkets like Home Plus (Tesco) have incorporated small, central food courts where shoppers can sit for a few minutes and grab a quick bite.

Odaeng is a fish cake that is boiled and served on a skewer. They are very cheap (usually 500 won) and are a common snack when walking around the markets. *Odaeng* is usually dipped in seasoned soy sauce and washed down with a cup of warm broth, which makes for a great pit stop on winter walks downtown.

Ddeok (tubular rice cakes) are simmered in a sweetened pepper sauce with strips of *odaeng* and boiled eggs to make **ddeokbokki**. Some twists on this popular favourite are to toss in fistfuls of shredded mozzarella cheese, or add *ramyeon* noodles to make **rapokki**. *Ddeokbokki* is especially popular among children and can usually be found within twenty paces of any elementary-, middle- or high school.

Twigim refers to battered, deep-fried foods reminiscent of Japanese tempura. In theory it can be anything, but the usual suspects are sweet potato, shrimp, squid, chilli pepper and pumpkin.

Sundae is a type of sausage stuffed with noodles, blood and various seasonings, and served with *samjang* paste and steamed pork liver. It doesn't win any beauty pageants, but lovers of blood sausage may more easily incorporate this popular favourite into their shopping expeditions.

To make **gimbap**, sticky rice is spread over a sheet of dried seaweed, other ingredients are laid across the top and it is rolled into a cylinder and cut into thick round slices. The fillings vary, but common ingredients are radish, egg, carrot, spinach and some kind of meat, like beef, imitation crab meat, tuna or chicken. This cheap, tasty snack is often eaten on the go, and is a common fixture of many impromptu picnics and school trips, and makes a satisfying light lunch for those with tight schedules.

Hoddeok is a flour pancake with a sweet, gooey mixture of brown sugar, cinnamon and nuts in the centre. Served hot off the griddle, it's hard to stop at just one. **Pungeobbang**

is a fish-shaped pastry filled with sweet red beans and will also satisfy a sweet tooth.

Vendors whip up *pungeobbang* and serve it warm off the griddle.

Like many Asian countries, Korea has its own take on the dumpling, which they call **mandu**. *Mandu* can be stuffed with just about anything, though popular fillings are minced, seasoned meat (*gogi mandu*), kimchi (*kimchi mandu*) or mixed vegetables (*yachae mandu*). They can be steamed (*jinmandu*), fried (*kunmandu*) or served in a broth (*manduguk*), and they vary in shape and size, from the daintier, snack-sized varieties, to the hefty *wangmandu* ("king mandu"), which is more of a meal.

Hot dog is the old American classic that takes different forms wherever it travels, and it deserves honourable mention in Korea, where the frank is boiled, skewered lengthwise, generously battered (and sometimes studded with French fries for good measure), deep fried and slathered with ketchup and mustard. This fusion treat is not recommended for hot dog purists, health fanatics or folks who mind having ketchup on their shirtfront for the rest of the day.

DINING ETIQUETTE

It's customary to wait to begin eating until the most senior member of your group is seated and has picked up his or her spoon and chopsticks. If you happen to be the most senior person and everyone around you seems to have suddenly lost their appetite, they're probably waiting for you to start or to indicate that they can feel free to dig in.

To begin the meal, the host or senior person will often say *Masitgae dusaeyo* (roughly translated as *Bon Appétit*!), to which the proper response is *Chalmeokgaessumnida*! ("[I] will eat well!") Among friends or business partners, you may hear the phrase "*Meonjeo dusaeyo*" ("You eat first"), in a show of polite deference which may go back and forth a few times until someone starts eating.

Many Korean restaurants provide silverware in a box on the table. One small way to show consideration or politeness is to offer the other people a set of utensils when you sit down.

After you've ordered your meal, Korean restaurant servers generally do not circulate around the dining room to periodically ask you if you need anything. You can flag your server by raising your hand and saying "*Yeogiyo*!" ("Here, please!"), or by pushing a call button that many restaurants have installed on the table.

At the Table

Every guidebook every written about Korea points out that you should not stand your chopsticks vertically in a bowl of rice, as this resembles the way incense is placed at funerals and memorial ceremonies. Perhaps there was a rash of chopsticks faux pas in the past, but I've never heard of anyone even feeling tempted to do this, and I only mention it on the off chance you or someone you know has a very particular method of playing with food.

Discrete, low-volume belching at the table is generally tolerated, though opinion is divided over noisy eating. Some don't seem to mind it, while others can't stand it. When in doubt, keep the volume down.

One thing to bear in mind is that it's generally not considered good manners to use a toothpick at the table. These are provided at the door and are used as you are leaving. Even then, it's good form to cover your mouth with your other hand.

If you need to blow your nose, don't do it at the table; excuse yourself and do it in the washroom.

To avoid an awkward situation of two people reaching for the last piece of *banchan*, Koreans leave the last piece, or request more from the staff.

In meat restaurants where you cook at the table, be mindful of who is manning the tongs and scissors. Offering to cook, particularly when one person has been doing it for a while, is a gesture that is appreciated. And it's kind of fun.

Even in restaurants where dishes are ordered individually, Koreans will often share. Can't decide if you want the carbonara or the risotto for lunch? Order both, ask your server for a couple of *apjeopsi* (extra dish), and dig in.

Soups can be served in individual bowls, or in large pots to be communally shared. Dipping one's spoon into a shared bowl of soup is fine. If that bothers you, many times a small side bowl will be provided if you'd like to portion some out to yourself, or just ask for one. One thing that will sometimes rub Koreans the wrong way is dipping a spoonful of rice into the soup to moisten and flavour it, even if the soup already contains rice, and even though it is the spoon, not the rice, that has been in and out of your mouth. If you like to flavour your rice with some of the soup (as I do on occasion), ladle it onto your rice in the rice bowl.

Koreans generally don't pick up their bowls when eating, and tend to stoop down low to eat if they have to. I admit to sometimes picking up my bowl at home when eating foods that may drip, and I have yet to be corrected for it, but it's best to avoid it when eating in more formal settings.

If someone older than you offers a drink, it's polite to accept it, even if you don't want it. When receiving it, use two hands or receive it in the right with the left hand supporting the right arm. In general, whenever anything is handed to you at the table, it's good to observe the two-hands rule.

It's common for the person who invites the other to pay, so be prepared to whip out the credit card if you are doing the inviting. Among friends and colleagues, it's common to reciprocate, and what goes around tends to come around. With younger people and larger groups, it's more common to split the check (what Koreans call "Dutch pay"), and restaurant staff will usually be happy to oblige.

After the meal it is polite to say to your host *Chalmeogeossumnida*! ("I ate well!"); but say it after the meal has been paid for. Saying it before the check is paid is a subtle way of asking the other person to pick up the tab.

A Final Note on Etiquette

This may seem like a lot to keep in mind, but Korean table etiquette quickly becomes second nature to many foreign residents in Korea. At any rate, one need not worry too much about making a faux pas; Koreans are generally pleased when they see foreigners taking an interest in Korean food, and sincere efforts to be polite go a long way.

DRINKING

Korean drinking culture stretches back well over a millennium, when their ancestors first began distilling alcoholic beverages. Their descendants today have a well-earned reputation as being among the hardest-drinking people in the world, as alcohol consumption, for better or worse, has been tightly woven into the tapestry of Korean life and society: as a way to build social bonds, celebrate holiday rituals, cement business relationships, loosen the tongue, pair with a meal, blow off steam after a long work day or simply to let one's hair down and party.

Koreans still enjoy many of their traditional brews and spirits, as well as a host of more recent arrivals from the West.

Soju

Soju is a clear distilled spirit made from potatoes or grains, though was traditionally made of rice. It's not as strong as other liquors (it ranges from about 10–25 per cent ABV), but

it packs a sneaky punch, as many diners at *samgyeopsal* restaurants have found their legs to be wobbly after knocking back a few glasses with dinner. Its potency, drinkability and price (less than 2,000 won a bottle) easily place *soju* in the biggest-bang-for-your-buck category, and have helped make it the most popular tipple in Korea, hands down. In recent years Koreans' love of the stuff made Jinro brand *soju* the top selling alcohol in the world—a remarkable fact considering that it is barely exported and is consumed mainly in Korea and Korean communities overseas.

Soju is usually drunk neat in a shot glass, though it mixes well and is often combined with fruit juices and sodas. One popular method is to make a *soju* boilermaker, or *poktanju* (from the word for bomb (*poktan*) and suffix -*ju*, which denotes any alcoholic drink) Just drop a shot of *soju* into a glass of beer and it's bombs away.

Makkeoli

Makkeoli is a cloudy, slightly effervescent rice wine that, like *soju*, is very inexpensive (under 2,000 won a bottle) and has ancient roots. Traditionally, *makkeoli* was the drink of farmers, but declined in popularity as Korea urbanised in the 1980s and 1990s. Lately, *makkeoli* has been enjoying something of a comeback, as college kids now consider it hip and can often be found crowding into many hole-in-the-wall *makkeoli jip* that are popping up around college campuses.

Makkeoli is sipped not from a glass but from a bowl, and is often paired with *pajeon* or *tubu kimchi* (kimchi tossed over seared tofu). While some may find the cheaper brands of store-bought *makkeoli* to be a bit rough, the better stuff is quite smooth and delicious, and at 6–8 per cent ABV gives you a real shot at making it home on your own two legs.

Beer

Since Koreans started brewing beer around a century ago, the Korean beer scene has been dominated by two major breweries (Hite-Jinro and Oriental Brewery (OB)) who long offered a mostly *soju*-drinking public a limited range of interchangeable lagers: one still occasionally sees this indifference in some of the older, provincial restaurants that list "beer" on the menu without bothering to identify the brand.

The big brewers still account for the lion's share of annual sales, but a change in government regulations in 2011 has allowed a vibrant craft beer scene to take root and grow in recent years, a development which is both a reflection of expanded tastes and a driver of new ones. Small local breweries now place their beers in pubs and taprooms around the country, considerably raising the bar for the big brewers and pushing them to up their game, while home brewing clubs, festivals and competitions have sprung up around the country and have gotten younger generations of Koreans genuinely excited about beer. The beer lover is coming to Korea at a good time, as it's no longer a trick to find a worthy stout, IPA, pilsner or Weizen to quench your thirst. Vive la Beer Revolution!

Wine

Wine has also become more widely available, and is imported from just about everywhere these days. Large supermarkets and specialty shops stock decent selections of wine at prices that have fallen into a reasonable range, though still a fair bit higher than what Europeans and North Americans may be used to. It's not nearly as popular as *soju* or even beer, but a passionate and growing local following have helped to make wine more accessible and enjoyable for the transplanted oenophile.

Anju

Whether it's a beer on the beach or a night on the town, Koreans almost always have some type of food to nibble on while they drink. Side dishes—called *anju*—can range from the simple and mundane to the hearty and exotic, and even the humblest drinking establishment will have a selection to choose from. Some types of alcohol have common pairings, while others can go with just about anything. Bar and pub staff used to insist that customers order food with their drinks, but these rules have greatly relaxed in recent years. Still, if you're going out with your Korean friends or colleagues, it's good to follow their lead and have something in your stomach.

Drinking Establishments

Koreans drink in a variety of places and settings, some of which will be familiar to foreign visitors, while others have a uniquely Korean twist.

Bars and pubs are more or less interchangeable, though a bar may have a slightly more lounge-y feel to it. These days they tend to have a wide selection of beer and spirits, as well as passable to excellent pub grub. Many bars and pubs also feature entertainment like darts, pool tables or table football (aka foosball) and a TV showing baseball, soccer or any international sporting event in which a Korean athlete is competing. Since the mid-aughts, Korea also boasts an increasing number of taprooms and brew pubs, in which the focus is more on beer, food and conversation that often seems to revolve around beer and food. Go figure.

A *makkeoli jip* is a place to sit down and drink *makkeoli* (what else?), usually while enjoying some variety of *jeon*, which makes for a time-honored pairing. *Makkeoli jip* tend to be cozy and more animated by voices than by loud music, and provide a welcome respite from rainy nights, office stress and whatever current K-pop hit is on endless loop at the bars.

Pojang macha are tented carts that serve alcohol and a variety of *anju*, and are earthy, unpretentious places where one can really feel *jeong*—the feeling of warmth and camaraderie between people who have common cause. *Soju* and Korean beer are the main beverages, but the *anju* they offer can be quite exotic and varied, from spicy chicken feet to cucumbers dipped in *samjang*. In the summer, the tent flaps are opened to give them a more *al fresco* feeling, and in the winter they come down for maximum warmth. Rain or shine, they usually open in the evening and can run into the wee hours and beyond, making them ideal for a beer after work, an intimate getting-to-know-you session after a dinner date, or as the last stop of a big night out.

Korea's pubs and taprooms offer beer lovers an ever-expanding array of quality brews.

From time to time, the Korean government has made attempts to close the *pojang macha* down or move them out of more visible, downtown areas, as they did during the 2002 FIFA World Cup, when they feared that *pojang macha* were unsightly and out-of-step with the modern image of Korea that they were trying to promote to the world. However, despite the ramshackle appearance and occasionally loose attention to hygiene standards, *pojang macha* ironically turned out to be quite a hit among foreign visitors, who often find them charming and authentic, and who frequently count those nights spent rubbing elbows with progressively uninhibited strangers among their fondest (if slightly fuzzy) memories of Korea.

Korea has no legal restrictions on drinking outdoors, and people do tend to make the most of it. Small gatherings in parks, on beaches and outside convenience stores (many of which now provide tables and seating) are a common sight around the country. Feel free to follow suit, but note that public trash bins can be hard to find, so be prepared to take your empties with you when you leave and dispose of them properly.

Dance clubs are similar to their Western counterparts, where guests are free to roam, dance, drink and mingle as they please. A "booking" club works a bit differently: patrons must have a table and are often expected to order *anju* as well as drinks, which can be quite pricey. If requested, the staff can perform a booking service—which means bringing together tables of men and women and letting them take it from there.

Room salons are male-only places that are staffed by attractive women who pour drinks, laugh at your attempts to be witty and provide varying degrees of "entertainment", which can mean anything from light petting to pairing off for the night. Normally the domain of businessmen and other high rollers, a trip to a room salon is sometimes part of what wining and dining a client or business partner involves.

"Host bars" cater to a female clientele, and are more or less the same as room salons but with the genders reversed, as young, handsome guys pamper female guests with attention of various kinds. Like room salons, they are extremely pricey, and are visited more as a special night out than as a regular haunt.

Noraebang means "singing room", and though it is strictly speaking not a drinking establishment, most singing rooms do serve alcohol to keep the party going and provide some liquid courage for your show-stopping, high-kicking rendition of *New York, New York*. Many nights out on the town with Koreans end up at a *noraebang* at some point, so if you are invited (or dragged) to one, fear not—the party may just be getting started.

One, Two, Cha Cha Cha!

A night out in Korea rarely begins and ends at the same place, but usually hits several places, which Koreans refer to with the counting unit cha. The first round (*il cha*) might start at a restaurant for dinner and a few preliminary drinks. Then you might move to a bar or pub (*i cha*) for a few more, and end up at a club, *noraebang*, or another bar for round three (*sam cha*). Depending on the group, you may hit anywhere from two to five spots—listen for your party's ringleader to announce "*i charo gapshida!*" ("Let's head to round two!")

Drinking Customs and Etiquette

As with dining etiquette, making an effort to do the right thing is what counts, and whatever gaffes you commit are even more likely to be forgiven when the booze is flowing and the mood is high.

Many of the cardinal rules of drinking in Korea concern the

pouring of drinks. It's customary to pour drinks for others, and is considered bad form to pour one's own drink. Use two hands when pouring for those older or more senior than you, either by holding the bottle with two hands, or by holding the bottle with the right hand while supporting the right arm below the elbow with the left hand. When pouring for peers or people less senior, use only the right hand to pour. Always pour for the eldest or most senior person first. After he or she is taken care of, pouring drinks for those who are younger or less senior than you is a classy touch.

Everyone seems to get the hang of that quickly enough, but what is slightly trickier is forming the habit of paying attention to the glasses of others, an easy thing to momentarily overlook in the flow of conversation and background buzz. Try not to let someone languish with an empty glass for too long, though if your friends are like mine, they will probably find a way (e.g., by coughing, tapping their glass or egging you to finish yours) to signal you to top them up. Also, don't refill a glass that isn't empty.

The same rules apply for receiving a drink: using two hands is more polite. When in doubt, it's better to err on the side of caution and use two hands, and leave it to your party to inform you if you are being excessively deferential.

When drinking with someone much older than you, it's considered polite to turn your head slightly to the side while you drink, though this custom appears to be on the wane. If you do find yourself in such a situation, take your cues from those around you, but understand that no one will fault you for failing to observe a custom that is no longer universally observed even among Koreans, while observing it may score you some points for refinement.

Korea can be tough on the teetotaller. When dining with

Korean work colleagues or business associates, some degree of drinking will be expected, and your ability to drink will be interpreted positively as a sign that you are willing to let your hair down and bond with the group. Refusing a drink outright is socially difficult, unless one cites religion or a health concern as the reason, either of which is accepted and understood.

If you have no such excuse, you're socially safer accepting at least the first drink—even if it is to merely raise it in a toast and symbolically touch it to your lips. Safer still is to drain the first glass, as it often accompanies a toast or speech from the most senior member of the group and is thus the most important round, and then either nurse or ignore the second glass for the rest of the evening. Bear in mind that an empty glass will quickly be refilled, but a glass containing alcohol will not, and will signal to your group that you're good for now.

If the leader of the group is a particularly heavy drinker or is laying on the pressure, you can usually placate him by either sipping your drink, or, if your timing is right, by turning sideways and discretely heaving it over your shoulder (being careful of course to glance downrange first). If at some point you must cry uncle, you won't be offending anyone by having given it your best, and may end up indirectly flattering your indefatigable host, who will have had the pleasure of drinking you under the table.

Conversely, if you are the type who enjoys tying one on now and then, you will suffer no shortage of drinking partners in Korea. "*Sul meokgo jukja!*" ("Let's drink and die!"), the rallying call of many a big night out, is not to be understood literally, but will often result in a progressively sloppy evening. If you do end up getting wobbly, the good news is that drunkenness itself carries virtually no social stigma, and unless you break the law or do something outrageous, all tends to be forgiven—if not forgotten—the following day.

Among businesspeople or more formal groups, a common term for "Cheers" is "*Wihayeo*!" which means "for the sake of", usually in reference to whatever speech or rallying cry has preceded it. More commonly, Koreans use the more informal "*Geonbae*" (literally, "empty glass") or "One shot," which in practical terms mean the same thing: bottoms up.

Drinking sessions in Korea are almost always accompanied with some sort of *anju*. Depending on the circumstances, *anju* could be anything from fried chicken to fruit to tortilla chips, but whatever it is, your Korean drinking buddies will

This bit of university graffiti captures the spirit of many nights out in Korea.

expect something. If you are
hosting the party, make sure the
group always has something to
nibble on.

Who Pays?

The old rule used to be that the
person who invites you pays the tab,
though like all things, this is in a state of
flux. Older Koreans or people in positions of relative authority
still tend to pay in those cases, and for you to insist on
paying in those cases risks offending your host (who often
will discretely pay without you knowing).

When going out in informal groups of friends, the general
rule is to "Dutch pay", the Konglish term for splitting the check
or running separate tabs. In small groups of close friends who
meet regularly, taking turns paying the tab is also practiced.
If that applies to your group, be ready to reciprocate when
the time comes.

Also note that tipping is not a custom in Korean restaurants and bars. Some pubs these days place tip jars on the bar, and small tips are appreciated but not expected.

CHAPTER 7

ENJOYING KOREA

> ❝To have friends come from afar,
> is that not also a joy?❞
>
> **— Confucius, *Analects***

South Korea's location in the heart of East Asia—once a historical liability—is a boon to travellers keen to explore Asia and points beyond, while the country also offers the domestic traveller a range of destinations, events and activities to keep you occupied on the peninsula.

GETTING IN AND OUT

Most visitors to Korea these days come in through Incheon International Airport, South Korea's stylish modern air hub, which looks as if it too had just recently descended from the clouds. The airport boasts fast arrival and departure rates, and various amenities including a sauna, sleeping rooms, golf, casino and a museum, which makes it almost a destination in itself, and are some of the reasons that it has regularly appeared at or near the top of the Passenger's Choice Awards for the past decade or so.

The former international airport, Gimpo, now serves as the primary domestic hub, though it also hosts a shuttle service to Tokyo. All large cities in Korea have an airport with connections to the capital and other domestic destinations. Jeju International Airport and Busan's Gimhae International Airport have connections to China, Japan, Taiwan and points in Southeast Asia.

For those with sturdy sea legs, a nice way to visit Korea's neighbours is to take a ferry. Fares are much cheaper than flying, and clearance through immigration and customs is generally much faster.

On the west coast, the international ferry terminals in Incheon and Pyeongtaek offer connections to roughly a dozen points in China, including Dalian, Qingdao and Weihai. On the east coast, the Busan International Ferry Terminal hosts several operators offering connections to Fukuoka, Shimonoseki and Osaka. There is currently one weekly ferry that makes the trip from Danghae to Vladivostok, and a possible reopening of the Sokcho-Zarubino-Vladivostok route also appears to be in the works.

South Korea shares its only land border (aka "The Demilitarized Zone") with North Korea, so at this writing (and for the foreseeable future) travellers can't freely leave or enter South Korea by land.

Travel to North Korea

Travel to North Korea is possible for citizens of any country except ROK passport holders, though the only way to visit the reclusive state is to book through a travel agency that specialises in North Korea tourism. You cannot travel independently in North Korea.

Despite the occasional flaring of tensions between North Korea and the US, a few thousand Western tourists visit North Korea every year, including many Americans, but one should be mindful of the risks and weigh them carefully before going. The US State Department currently advises strongly against travel to North Korea due to the "serious risk of arrest and long-term detention" for relatively minor offenses. About a dozen Americans have been detained in North Korea in the past decade, the latest of which was Otto Warmbier, a university student who was accused of stealing a poster from a Pyongyang hotel in January 2016 and was sentenced to fifteen years in a hard labour camp, where he remains nearly ten months later at this writing.

GETTING AROUND KOREA

South Korea has an excellent system of transportation. User-friendly, efficient and cheap, Korea's trains and buses can get you pretty much anywhere you want to go, and have greatly reduced or obviated the need to own a car of one's own.

Train

Korea has three classes of trains. The cheapest are the Mugunghwa trains, which make many stops, and are thus generally used for traveling between nearby cities and towns. A step up from these are the Saemaeul trains, which cost more and are a faster way to travel longer distances.

For intercity travel however, the KTX leaves both of these in the dust. Cruising at 200 km/hour, the KTX runs from Seoul down two major lines: the Gyoungbu line departs from Seoul Station and makes stops in points southeast, terminating in Busan; and the Honam line runs southwest, connecting Seoul's Yongsan Station with Mokpo.

Tickets can be booked in person at any station, or online at www.letskorail.com. Unlimited Korea Rail passes are also available at reasonable rates for those who want to cover a lot of ground in a short time.

Bus

Nearly every city in Korea has an intercity bus terminal, so if you are headed to a smaller city that is not served by a rail line, you can take usually an intercity bus. Bus fares are cheap, and the buses are the air-conditioned coach variety. Bus tickets can be a little trickier for foreigners to book online because of the relative lack of English-language information, but heading down to a bus terminal ticket counter in person (or with a Korean friend) can do the trick. Be aware that intercity traffic is heavy during holidays (especially Chuseok and Seollal), and seats should be booked well in advance.

Ferry

Most Korean coastal cities of any size have ferry terminals with daily connections to nearby islands. Except for major holidays, they seldom sell out, and I've never had a problem booking in person on the day of travel.

Car

Driving in Korea is a good option if you'd like to set your own pace, plot a more specific route, and explore hard-to-reach places. An excellent system of roads and expressways can get you anywhere fast, provided that traffic is cooperative. During national holidays or peak summer season (late July/early August), intercity traffic can slow to a crawl, and tends to make just about any other mode of transport seem a more sensible and appealing option. But for jaunts into the countryside, many folks find driving to be the best way to go.

ACCOMMODATION

Korea offers a variety of accommodation options for travellers of every budget and inclination.

Four-star hotels (like Hyatt, Westin, Lotte and Novotel) are found in major cities and have the same amenities you would expect to find at comparable hotels anywhere. Luxury **resorts** are scattered around the country, and are sometimes linked to golf courses, ski slopes, spas and other attractions.

Motels can be found everywhere in Korea, and range from cheap and spartan to pricey and well-appointed. They tend to cluster in entertainment/nightlife areas and can usually be reserved easily for anywhere from 30,000 to over 100,000 won a night won depending on the quality.

A *yeogwan* is an older style of accommodation that is similar to motels in their general layout, amenities and price range, though many *yeogwans* these days are rebranding themselves as motels, which are generally perceived be of slightly higher quality (and thus command higher room rates). Some *yeogwans* offer *ondol* rooms, which forgo beds in favour of mats and comforters to be spread out over a heated floor, an arrangement that is still popular among large groups and families who want to share a room and crash the old-fashioned way.

A **minbak** is another older and simpler form of accommodation that is more common in the countryside. Essentially, *minbak* accommodation is staying in someone's home for a small fee, and usually includes a home-cooked meal or two. Some of the larger *minbak* resemble a small inn, with the proprietor living on the premises or adjacent. *Minbak* are a cozy and intimate way to explore rural Korea, if you can find one: they appear to be on the path to extinction due the rise of modern accommodation options.

Guesthouses and **B&Bs** are more modern versions of the *minbak*, and they often get lumped together because of their similarities, though B&Bs tend to be a bit trendier, more expensive and may feature better food and amenities. For a unique experience, you can try staying in a **hanok guesthouse**. *Hanok* refers to the traditional Korean house, which is currently enjoying a revival of interest and popularity, both as a form of accommodation and cultural experience. Some areas, like Seoul's historic Bukchon village, feature many gracefully-restored *hanok* where tourists can revisit the past in comfort and in style.

The rise of **pension**-style accommodation in the countryside is also partly responsible for the decline of the *minbak*, as many folks seem to prefer something a bit newer, cleaner and more convenient. Pensions feature a private bathroom and kitchen and often have an *ondol*-style sleeping arrangement, making them popular with groups or families.

Korea has a growing network of **hostels**, and can be a cheap way to travel around Korea for extended periods, but by far the cheapest way to travel around Korea is to stay at a ***jjimjilbang*** (sauna), many of which are open 24-hours and feature large, common, *ondol*-style sleeping areas. Saunas may charge anywhere from 4,000 to 20,000 won, provide you with shorts and a top to wear during your stay, and don't charge extra if you decide to sleep there.

PUBLIC HOLIDAYS

Korean public holidays are scattered around the calendar, and offer visitors the chance to experience various facets of Korean culture, as well as the time off to enjoy them.

New Year's Day (1 January) – Koreans mark the New Year by the solar as well as the lunar calendar. On 1 January (by the solar calendar), many people wake early to see the sunrise, while others find it easier to stay out all night and see it before heading home.

Jeju island sunrise

Lunar New Year (late Jan/early February) – The Lunar New Year, or Seollal, is a three-day holiday centred on the first day of the first lunar month, and is one of biggest holidays in Korea along with Chuseok (see below). Though many folks are increasingly treating Seollal as a time to relax at home or take a short trip, many Koreans still celebrate it in a more-or-less traditional way: by visiting the family patriarch or matriarch and performing a deep bow called *sebae* to show respect (and in exchange for a little pocket money, called *sebae don*). As on Chuseok, they perform an ancestor memorial ceremony called *charye* (see below), and enjoy a big meal together.

One food particularly associated with Seollal is *ddeokguk*, a soup made from sliced long rice cakes which symbolise longevity—according to tradition, you are counted as one year older only after you have eaten your *ddeokguk* on Seollal. Some folks play traditional games like *yutnori* (a board game played by throwing four sticks to determine the number of moves one can make), though these days they are probably just as likely to be plugged into a smartphone playing the latest app game. Stores can be very crowded in the run-up to Seollal, as people go to buy gifts and food to prepare for the elaborate *charye* table.

Korean Age

It's common to hear people say things like, "My international age is 34, but my Korean age is 36," causing some foreigners to wonder if they've travelled through a time warp to get here. Fear not: the reason for the discrepancy is simply that Koreans reckon age a little differently. In Korea, you are considered one year old at birth, and you age one year every Lunar New Year along with everyone else. For foreigners, giving your age Korean style sometimes takes a bit of getting used to, especially as you draw near the milestone birthdays (30, 40, 50, etc) and are not crazy about the idea of crossing that threshold any sooner than you need to. When people ask you casually, you can give your age any way you like, but for official purposes, or in cases where someone wishes to know whether they need to address you as an elder, junior or peer, any potential confusion is immediately cleared up by asking you your birth year.

Independence Movement Day (1 March) – *Sam-il jeol* means "Three-one day" and refers to 1 March 1919, when Korean Independence activists formally proclaimed independence from Japan in the first major act of resistance to Japanese colonisation of Korea. Today, the event is commemorated with a public reading of their Declaration of Independence in Pagoda Park in Seoul.

Children's Day (5 May) – Children's Day also has its roots in the Japanese colonial period, when publisher and social activist Bang Jeong-hwan organised a day focused on improving the welfare of Korea's children and instilling in them a sense of their national identity. Since 1970, Children's Day has been a public holiday, and is a time for parents to spend quality time with their kids.

Buddha's Birthday (eighth day of the fourth lunar month; falls in May), or *Bucheonim oshin nal*, celebrates the coming of the Buddha, which is what the Korean name means ("the day Buddha came"). Buddha's birthday is one of Korea's most colourful holidays, as temples around the country are festooned with lotus lanterns, making a visit to one a visual treat. Inside the lanterns, temple visitors hang paper tags bearing a wish or a prayer to the Buddha, and everyone who makes the trip enjoys a free meal of *bibimbap*.

Buddhist temples, like Busan's Yonggungsa (pictured here), provide solace from the urban bustle, as well as visual treats both large and small.

Memorial Day (6 June) was established to honour and commemorate the fallen of the Korean War and other conflicts. Remembrance ceremonies are held at the National Cemetery in Seoul and the UN cemetery in Busan, and citizens are encouraged to take a few minutes to offer gratitude or silent prayers to all those who made the ultimate sacrifice.

Liberation Day (15 August) marks the end of colonial rule in Korea after Japan's defeat in the Second World War in 1945, and has the distinction of being the only holiday celebrated by both North and South Korea, though under different names. In the North, it is *Chogukhaebangeuinal* ("Liberation of the Fatherland Day"), and in the South it is called *Gwangbokjeol* ("The Day the Light Returned").

Chuseok (15th day of the eighth lunar month) is a three-day harvest festival celebrated in mid-autumn, and like many harvest festivals around the world, it is a time to express thanks to the forces that have given us life and prosperity, which in Korea means honouring one's ancestors. On Chuseok, many Koreans perform an ancestral rite called *charye*. Though it may take different forms, a *charye* ceremony involves a ceremonial table/shrine laden with a bounty of food, offerings of libation to the ancestors and the deepest of bows (called *sebae*) before the ceremonial table to express one's profound respect and gratitude. Traditionally, Koreans migrated to their ancestral hometowns to celebrate Chuseok, and many still do so, but in modern times, many others are opting for a simplified observance of the holiday, or simply using it to catch up on some R-and-R.

National Foundation Day (3 October) – When talking about a peninsula that has seen many dynasties come and go over a period of several millennia, one has to be clear about which "nation" one is referring to. National Foundation Day commemorates the founding, not of the modern Republic of Korea, but of the first proto-Korean kingdom (Gojoseon) by Dangun in 2333 BC. There are some official observances, but for most folks, it's just a welcome day off from work.

Christmas (25 December) – Apart from the religious observances by Korea's many Christians, Christmas has also caught on as a secular/commercial holiday, though the outward trappings tend to be more muted than in some Western countries. For many foreign residents, Christmas can be a tough time to be away from family, so many expats celebrate it together in one way or another: Christmas parties, Secret Santas, or a fridge full of eggnog has helped many a homesick *waegukin* beat the holiday blues.

Valentine's Day

For the past few decades, young Korean couples have observed Valentine's Day on 14 February, though with a Korean twist: women give chocolate to men as a sign of their interest or affection. Men reciprocate on White Day (14 March), another cultural import created by Japanese confectioners in the 1970s, by giving chocolates or lollipops to the ladies. Those who were left out of the gift-giving may observe Black Day on 14 April, which is "celebrated" by eating *jajjangmyeon* (noodles in black bean sauce), either alone or with a similarly lovelorn friend.

Korea's various foreign communities have many of their own traditions and events to commemorate the holidays of their home countries. Some others of note are St Patrick's Day, Halloween, Canada Day, ANZAC Day, US Independence Day, US and Canadian Thanksgiving, Boxing Day and Cinco de Mayo.

FESTIVALS

Korea has a variety of festivals large and small, with new ones added seemingly every year. The following is a list of some of the bigger, more famous or otherwise notable festivals around Korea.

Boryeong Mud Festival – What started out as a fun if messy way to promote locally-produced, mud-infused cosmetics has turned into an annual event that attracts over two million visitors to this small west coast city every

July. The Boryeong Mud Festival is almost considered a rite of passage for many foreigners, and has what is often described as a frat party atmosphere. Beyond partying, the festival features many events, the gist of which boils down to getting as covered in mud as possible.

A masked performer at the Andong Mask Dance Festival.

Andong Mask Dance Festival – Chief among the many traditional cultural attractions in Andong is the Mask Dance Festival, an event spanning several days that features traditional dances by performers in elaborate masks that portray a few stock characters (the aristocrat, the scholar, the monk, the fool, the grandmother, etc), as well as performances by dance troupes from around the world. Visitors can also try their hand at creating masks and other handcrafts, or simply take in the sights of Andong and Hahoe Village, living museums in themselves where Korea's Confucian heart beats most audibly.

Busan International Film Festival (BIFF) – Currently in its 21st year, the Busan international Film Festival tends to focus on young filmmakers from around Asia, though several big names from abroad attend every year: past visitors include Wim Wenders, Harvey Keitel, Quentin Tarantino and Oliver Stone. The epicentre is the space-agey Cinema Center in Busan's Centum City, with several screenings at cinemas around town. BIFF is good chance to get a sense of what's new in Asian cinema, and to get away from the regular box office fare, but book your tickets in advance.

Jinhae Cherry Blossom Festival – In late March or early April, cherry blossoms bloom in the southern part of the Korean peninsula, and many people flock to Jinhae to enjoy the sight of streets shaded in canopies of pink and white. The festival draws an estimated two million people, so if the timing of the blossoms permits, a weekday visit is advised to avoid the worst of the crowds. Jeju Island also hosts a cherry blossom festival, which arrives earlier than in other parts of the peninsula.

Summer is a time for music festivals in Korea. The **Jisan Valley Rock Festival** in July features many of Korea's top rock bands and some heavyweights from around the world. **Pentaport Rock Festival**, held in Incheon over three days in late July, is another big one, and has featured acts like Weezer, Travis, The Prodigy and Suede. The **Busan International Rock Festival** is a smaller festival with more of a focus on Korean bands, but has also attracted an eclectic range of foreign performers, from Steve Vai to Cannibal Corpse. In October, the **Jarasum International Jazz Festival** draws top international performers and over 200,000 fans of jazz and world music to a small river island in the town of Gapyeong for three days of music and camping.

Jindo Sea-Parting Festival – Between March and April, extreme low tides in the East China Sea off Korea's southwest coast expose a 2.9-km land bridge between the islands on Jindo and Modo, a natural phenomenon that a former French ambassador to Korea dubbed Korea's version of the "Moses Miracle". The event is celebrated in an annual festival in Hoedong Village that features a variety of cultural activities, local foods and the surreal spectacle of thousands of people appearing to walk across the sea.

Cheongdo Bullfighting Festival – Every spring in Cheongdo, bulls are squared off against other bulls in the Cheongdo Bullfighting Festival, a popular event that recalls the centuries-old tradition of farmers pitting their prized oxen against one another. Animal lovers can take consolation in knowing that unlike in Spanish bullfighting, the bull is never killed, and the fight is over when one bull turns tail and concedes.

Seoul hosts an **International Fireworks Festival** in October along the Han River, featuring a series of dazzling pyrotechnics by Korean and award-winning international fireworks creators. Busan also hosts a large fireworks show in late October at Gwanganli Beach. Both events are very well attended, so arrive early to get a closer spot, or ask around for other vantage points away from the crowds.

One of the many larger-than-life relief panoramas at the Haeundae Sand Festival

Every May, the sand at Busan's Haeundae Beach serves as the medium for dozens of artists, who transform the 1.5-km strand into a sculpture garden featuring dragons, mermaids, temples, cartoon characters and other fanciful designs during the **Haeundae Sand Festival**. You'll never look at a sandcastle the same way again.

Jagalchi Fish Market, one of the largest and oldest fish markets in Korea, hosts the **Busan Jagalchi Festival** every October, which centres around eating lots of fresh seafood

Boseong tea fields

and events like cooking contests and eel races. Seafood lovers, take note.

The main event at the **Hwacheon Sancheoneo Ice Festival** (held in January in Hwacheon, Gangwon Province) is drilling a hole through 40 cm of ice in search of some delectable *sancheoneo* (mountain trout), and then setting up a barbecue on the banks to grill your catch and bring sensation back to your extremities.

Tea lovers and shutterbugs may enjoy the **Boseong Green Tea Festival**, where you can sample locally-grown green tea and tea-related products in one of Korea's more photogenic places: the terraced tea fields snaking around the hills of Boseong.

HOBBIES, SPORTS AND ACTIVITIES

Korea has often been described as a "work hard, play hard" society, and as the label suggests, there are a variety of sports and leisure activities on offer, both indoors and out.

Paduk is often played outdoors by older men, and usually draws a gaggle of onlookers and commentators.

Games

Koreans are big fans of games, both modern and traditional. Many older folks play games like *paduk* or *janggi*, and you may often see them in parks spread out on a blanket, usually with one or two onlookers enjoying a tense matchup between two old hands. Card games of many kinds are also popular among many middle-aged Koreans. Some common games are *hula*, *hwatu*, and increasingly, poker. Though gambling is technically illegal, many people host quiet poker games with friends or acquaintances, and there are even poker rooms that pop up from time to time and can be found by asking around. Poker players can also visit the Seven Luck Casino in Seoul, which at this writing has a regular Texas Hold'em table.

For younger Koreans, gaming tends to not involve cards or dice but electronics. Phone app games immensely popular, and you will often see young Koreans blasting away on their devices as they walk down the street, skilfully dodging virtual hazards while occasionally stumbling into actual ones. Those who prefer the older style of gaming may like to check out a Board Game Room, which stock many old standards and can usually be found in university districts.

PC gaming has been especially popular since the late 1990s, when games like *Starcraft* and first-person shooters like *Rainbow Six* were the rage, and many Koreans from 14 to 40 still flock to PC bangs to play the latest titles. True to the group ethos, the most popular games tend not to be console games like X-Box and Playstation (which people tend to play alone at home) but games that can be played multi-player, either online or in local area networks. If you want a challenge, accompany a Korean friend to a PC room and prepare to receive a free schooling in your game of choice.

PC gaming in Korea is also a serious professional pursuit and a spectator "e-sport", in which the top players in games like *League of Legends* earn big salaries through corporate sponsorships and enjoy celebrity status. Big tournaments are held in stadiums and are televised, while fans and commentators knowingly discuss the ins and outs of strategies as one would with any sport.

Noraebang

Karaoke fans have come to the right country, as Koreans young and old enjoy belting out the latest ballads in *noraebangs* ("Singing rooms") around the country. Many adults head to a *noraebang* as part of a night out, businesspeople head to *noraebangs* as one more way of bonding with clients and colleagues, and school kids crowd into smaller booth-style *noraebangs* at game rooms and croon along with the current K-pop hits.

As the name suggests, customers get their own private rooms, so the only audience are the people who came with you and whatever poor souls on the adjacent floors. Rates are cheap and usually run in the neighbourhood of 10,000–15,000 won per hour. Most also serve drinks, snacks and other refreshments, so the party doesn't have to stop. However you feel about yourself as a singer, note that the *noraebang* atmosphere is very forgiving: vocals are often drenched in reverb, remote controls allow you to change the keys of songs to get them within your vocal range and a shot or two of liquid courage all help to ensure that even your most wobbly efforts will be applauded.

Saunas and Public Baths

The *mogyoktang* (public bath) and *jjimjilbang* (sauna) are affordable luxuries that were one of the first things I fell in love with in Korea: for about the price of a movie ticket, they are great places to unwind, beat a hangover, escape the noise or just pamper yourself for a while.

Though they vary in the particulars, *mogyoktangs* have separate facilities for men and women featuring hot and cold tubs, a shower area, a sometimes a steam room or dry sauna. There is also usually a rest area where guests can watch TV and buy soft drinks. Other features can include an exfoliating body scrub service for an extra charge (not for the timid), a barber, pools with various water jets and a variety of mineral-infused hot baths. Small, neighbourhood *mogyoktangs* still tend to be cheap (around 3,000–6,000 won), while the more luxurious ones usually won't set you back more than 20,000 won, and in either case, you can stay as long as you like.

If you're worried about other patrons gawking at you, don't be. Foreigners may still draw some curious looks, particularly out in the country or in smaller out-of-the-way urban neighbourhoods, but in most cases you will not be the novelty you would have been years ago.

Unlike the bathhouses, *jjimjilbangs* are not segregated by gender, so patrons are given loose-fitting shorts and shirts to wear. *Jjimjilbangs* feature various types of dry sauna rooms (many of which have special properties with various alleged health benefits), and common areas to lounge around, eat snacks, watch TV, read comics or crash out on a heated floor. On weekends, many Korean families, friends and couples head there for some quality down time. These days, many *jjimjilbangs* are part of a larger complex that may include a gym, swimming pool, bathhouse, yoga classroom and such, and can vary in price depending on which of the facilities you want to use.

Fitness

Haelseu jang (health clubs) and fitness centres of various kinds can be found all over Korea at a range of prices. Many offer classes in anything from spinning to Zumba to yoga, and may have facilities for squash, racquetball, swimming and climbing. Crossfit has a foothold as well, and gyms can be found in every major city.

SPECTATOR SPORTS

Koreans are avid sports fans, especially during international competitions when Korean athletes compete on the world stage. Domestically, the most popular spectator sport is baseball, with soccer a distant second and basketball an even more distant third.

The Korean Baseball Organization (KBO) currently features ten teams based in cities around the peninsula. The level of play is a notch or two below the US Major Leagues, but it is a competitive league that over the years has nonetheless produced some standout MLB players, as well as hosted many former MLB players from North and South America who have added a lot of pop, colour and excitement to the game.

Tickets are much cheaper than their MLB counterparts, and the stadium atmosphere is an experience in itself, even for those who know little and care less about the game. Cheerleaders, beer, fried chicken, manic mascots and thousands of fans singing, chanting and taunting in unison make for an unforgettable experience.

K-League Soccer has a tough time competing against the KBO (whose season runs more or less concurrently) and the European soccer leagues (which siphon off the best Korean players and dominate the airwaves), but they can be fun to attend live. Currently there are 23 teams divided into a first and second division, and the best teams are eligible for the AFC Champions League, which sees the best teams in Asia square off.

The Korean Basketball League (KBL) is relatively new (established in 1997) and features ten teams. The KBL struggles to draw big crowds, but for fans of live basketball, it's the best game in town.

Sports to Play

There are a variety of sports to play in South Korea for folks interested in getting off the bench. Various team sports are organised into leagues, often mixed with Koreans and foreigners and can be a good way to get your sports fix and make local friends. Scanning Facebook groups or local publications and websites are the best way to turn up info. Some of the sports that are available are baseball, soccer,

Gaelic football

rugby, Gaelic football, ultimate frisbee, golf (and screen golf), tennis, ice hockey and ball hockey, volleyball, bowling, darts and American football.

Korea also has a variety of martial arts available for learners of all ages. Many instructors will have limited English, which gives you a great opportunity to learn Korean at the same time you are learning your punches, kicks and throws. The following is a list of the most common martial arts practiced in Korea.

Taekwondo is a Korean martial art developed in the 20th century as a form of self-defense, and is very popular in Korea. The focus of the style is reflected in the name: *tae* ("kick") + *kwon* ("punch") + *do* ("the way of").

Similar to Japanese *aikido*, *hapkido* is a martial art that focuses on pressure points, joint locks and throws, and seeks to use the opponent's momentum as a means of control. These classes are also popular and relatively easy to find.

Geomdo is a traditional sword art that may focus on form or sparring or both.

Other martial arts that are available in Korea are judo, *wushu* (*kung fu*), tai chi, kickboxing, Muay Thai, boxing and *kuksulwon*, which is a blend of various Korean martial arts traditions.

OUTDOOR SPORTS AND ACTIVITIES

Korea's geography and temperate climate guarantee that outdoor types can find plenty to do year-round.

Hiking and Trekking

In a country that is 70 per cent mountains, hiking is a natural and very popular way to enjoy the outdoors, as Korea's rugged topography ensures that you are never far from a hiking trail, even in large cities, which often contain miles of hiking trails within city limits. On weekends, many Koreans gear up and head to the hills for anything from serious treks to casual jaunts ending in a picnic at some scenic spot. Popular trails can get busy at certain times of year, but hiking is generally a great way to beat the crowds, get some exercise, see the country and get some fresh air.

Korea has far too many trails to list, and everyone has their favourites, but most of the popular routes centre around the more notable peaks, like Jirisan, Hallasan, Soraksan, Bukhansan and others. Hikers of all levels can find something to suit their desired degree of difficulty, and the views in any season never disappoint.

Jeju Island's Olle Trail (*Olle gil*) has lately become a must for anyone serious about seeing Korea on foot. Opened in 2007, the Olle Trail comprises a connected series of 21 main routes at this writing and several sub-routes that take

Korea's many small islands (like Memuldo, pictured here) are very scenic and make for some great hikes.

trekkers past farms, orchards, villages, coastline and many of Jeju's famous *oreum*, the many small parasitic volcanoes that dot the landscape.

In recent years, city planners around Korea have laid down many miles of well-used running/walking paths in parks and along riversides, which has made walking, jogging and cycling a much safer and more pleasant experience.

Sailing

If mountains are not your thing, another way to get away from the crowds is by sea, or in the case of Seoul, by river. The Seoul Marina Club and Yacht, just south of the Han River in Yeouido, offers rentals, charters and lessons. Across the river, the Seoul 700 Yacht Club maintains several boats for members to use, and also offers lessons to both members

A recreational sailor angles his dinghy toward Busan's Gwangan Bridge.

and non-members. Check their website (www.700yachtclub.com/eng/main.htm) for current rates and information.

Down south, the Busan Expat Sailing Club, located at the Sooyoungman Marine near Busan's Haeundae Beach, offers lessons, charters, rentals and lessons for sailors of all skill levels. Visit their website (www.busansailing.com) for details.

Fishing

As you might expect on a peninsular country that is intersected by many rivers and streams, both salt-water and freshwater fishing are popular pastimes in Korea. Popular spots can get quite crowded, but a little hunting around will often result in finding a good place to try your luck. Around the coast, Korean salt-water anglers ply the seawalls and beaches, and often hire local fisherman to drop them on a small islet for the day and pick them up later. In coastal cities like Incheon, Busan, Ulsan, Pohang and on Jeju Island, it's also possible to charter boats to take you out for the day. Some common species include mackerel, mullet, flounder, yellowtail, sea bass, porgy and various species of bream.

Fans of freshwater fishing can also find various opportunities around the country. Bass were introduced to Korea in the late 20th century, and can be found in nearly all of the country's rivers and streams. Because they are not table fish and are thus not valued as highly as the salt-water species, they tend to be under-fished and can grow to eye-popping sizes.

Korean streams are also home to a variety of much sought-after trout: lenok (aka Manchurian trout), cherry trout and non-native populations of rainbows. Because these are more sought-after than bass (and because there are currently no regulations or licences for freshwater fishing) few are able to grow to full maturity. However, devoted fly-fishers report that good spots await those willing to look for them in the Baekdudaegan

Sport fishermen are a common sight up and down the Korean coast.

mountain range, the spiny ridge that runs the length of the peninsula and is home to the country's trout streams.

Water Sports

At beaches around the country, there are a variety of water sports on offer: snorkelling, paddle boarding, water skiing, jet skiing and parasailing. Surfing has become popular along Korea's east coast, though the waves may not always be up to snuff. Surfers report that the beaches of Gangwon-do, Pohang, Busan and Jeju Island will give you your best shot at riding decent waves, especially during winter or when a big storm is blowing in the region.

Cycling

It wasn't long ago that cyclists in Korea had to take their lives in their hands and negotiate hazardous roads and crowded sidewalks to get from A to B. In recent years, however, as cycling has grown in popularity, heavy investment by local and regional governments in cycling infrastructure has produced a friendlier riding environment. Nearly every river of any size now has dedicated bike trails, enabling riders to cruise scenic areas in safety while escaping the manic bustle of the streets.

Jeju Island has many miles of biking trails that circle and crisscross the island and allow for some very pleasant and scenic riding. The crown jewel of Korea's riding trails is the Four Rivers (*Sa Daegang*) cycling trail, a 620-kilometre marked trail that stretches from Incheon in the northwest to Busan in the southeast. Only 30 per cent of the trail is shared with cars (and these sections tend to be small rural roads), while the rest is dedicated to cyclists, with plenty of scenery and amenities for camping, food and bike repair

자전거전용

여기서부터 1,2km

Dedicated bike lanes, like this one in a Busan university district, are an increasingly common sight in Korean cities.

along the way. South Korea's hills and mountains also offer ample opportunities for mountain biking, and trails can be found all over the country.

Camping

Camping is another way of putting the city behind you for a few days and enjoying the Korean countryside. The size of Korea and the population density make it hard to find truly remote areas, but a little searching (and a willingness to go during off-peak times) can get you some peace and quiet.

Campers in Korea have a few options for getting their nature fix. One is to visit a commercial campsite, which are usually located in national parks. These can be convenient for people with little camping experience, as they provide tents, running water and electricity, but they can also be crowded, noisy and hard to book, particularly in summer. Though not

DARLING WE'RE CAMPING!

TRIGG.

exactly what you would call "getting away from it all", these can be fun for those craving a more social experience.

For those who want to get a bit further away, there are other options. Most beaches in Korea allow camping, and while these too can get crowded in summer, they are very quiet for most of the rest of the year. Wild camping is also possible, and Korea's mountains offer abundant places for determined campers to pitch tents for the night. Camping on the beach or in the mountains is legal, and is tolerated as long as campers observe the same basic rules that apply everywhere: respect your surroundings, and don't leave anything behind.

Those who don't like the idea of roughing it might also like to try glamping ("glamorous camping"), a trend which has caught on in Korea and can be found around the country. "Glampsites" feature well-appointed tents with cozy bedding, and sites are often equipped with such creature comforts as wifi, hot showers, barbecue pits, air-conditioning and swimming pools. Book in advance, as these too fill up in the summer.

Skiing and Snowboarding

In recent years, winter sports have become popular in Korea and have gained a growing and devoted following. Korea's topography and climate are well-suited for winter sports, and with the coming of the Winter Olympics to Pyeongchang in 2018, growing infrastructure has enabled many more residents to enjoy skiing, snowboarding, sledding and ice skating than ever before.

Most of Korea's ski resorts are located in Gangwon Province, and many are within striking distance of Seoul, so that day trips and weekend trips are fairly easy, while those coming up from points south may want to make a weekend of it. The slopes can be crowded at peak times, but as new trails and resorts are being added all the time, it's becoming increasingly possible to find the space to carve some fresh lines. Some popular spots are Yongpyong Resort, Phoenix Park, Alpensia Resort (the main venue for the 2018 Winter Olympics), Jisan Forest Resort and Daemyung Vivaldi Park.

Ice Skating

Ice skating is a popular activity in South Korea, and many Korean cities have indoor skating rinks that operate year round. Rentals are cheap, but those who need larger sizes may want to be safe and bring their own skates. Peak times are during school vacations, so plan accordingly or be prepared to be surrounded by legions of kids aspiring to be the next Kim Yuna or Viktor Ahn.

Jeju Island's volcanic origin lends its coastline a rugged beauty.

CHAPTER 8

LEARNING THE LANGUAGE

> *If you talk to a man in a language he understands, that goes to his head. If you talk to him in his own language, that goes to his heart.*

— Nelson Mandela

The Korean language (alternately called *hangukeo* or *hangukmal*) was once thought to be a part of a proposed language family called Altaic that was believed to include Turkish, Mongolian, Japanese and a few others, but this theory no longer holds sway. Most linguists now consider Korean to be in a family of its own (The Koreanic group) and whose only relatives are now extinct.

Korean is the official language of both North and South Korea, though the two have some significant differences. Some linguists consider the Korean dialect spoken in Jeju to be a distinct language that is related to Korean and which together constitute a small language family. However they are officially classified, the two are mutually unintelligible and strike even the untrained ear as being very different. Standard Korean is universally understood by Jeju natives, who learn it in school, but the opposite is not true of mainland Koreans, who report being utterly mystified by the local tongue when they visit Jeju on holiday.

CHALLENGES IN LEARNING KOREAN

Some features of Korean don't present special challenges for foreign learners. Unlike tonal languages, Korean intonation is flat and doesn't require the vocal acrobatics of languages like Thai, Vietnamese and Mandarin. Apart from a handful of tricky vowels and consonants, the sounds of Korean tend not to be hard for English speakers to approximate. And thanks to the efforts of King Sejong, Korean no longer depends on modified Chinese characters for its written expression, but is rendered by an elegant, phonetic alphabet called *Hangeul* that can be mastered by anyone in a couple of days.

Having said that, Korean does have many features that hinder and confound foreign learners, which is the reason the US State Department's Foreign Service Institute and others rate it as one of the hardest languages to master. For starters, Korean syntax follows a subject-object-verb order, so that in Korea, the boy doesn't eat an apple, the *boy apple eats*. This is easy enough to wrap one's head around in simple sentences, but can get very confusing as sentences lengthen and clauses pile up in the seemingly wrong direction, all while you wait for that final verb that pins it all together.

Korean vocabulary can be tough as well. Over the centuries, Koreans have been very liberal in borrowing words from other languages: over half of Korean vocabulary comes from Chinese, either as a direct loan word, or as a Koreanised version of a Chinese character (which Koreans call *Hanja* and still use today in limited contexts). More recently, English has been the source of many new Korean words, so that after getting used to the pronunciation shift, the beginning foreign student is pleased to find that he or she has no trouble figuring out what is meant by *compyuteo* (computer), *haembeogeo* (hamburger) or *miniseukeoteu* (miniskirt). But unlike the Romance or Germanic languages, which abound in cognates that English speakers will recognise and draw on to decipher and recall new words, Korean vocabulary bears no useful resemblance to the lexicons of other languages. You may find, as I and many others did, that while you cannot for example forget the Spanish word for restaurant (*restaurante*) even if you tried, it may take a considerable amount of drilling for *sikdang* to penetrate the old cranium.

Korean numbers present special problems, which is unfortunate because they so often come up in daily life in the form of bills, restaurant checks, clocks, invoices, calendars, contracts and so on. The first hurdle is that Korean has two systems of numbers, a native Korean number system, and a Sino-Korean one.

NUMBER	SINO-KOREAN	KOREAN NUMBER
1	*il*	*hana*
2	*i*	*dul*
3	*sam*	*saet*
4	*sa*	*naet*
5	*o*	*taseot*
6	*yuk*	*yeoseot*
7	*chil*	*ilgop*
8	*pal*	*yeodol*
9	*gu*	*ahop*
10	*sip*	*yeol*
11	*sip-il*	*yeol-hana*
20	*i-sip*	*seumul*
30	*sam-sip*	*seoreun*

Once you've learned both sets, you then discover that they are used in different contexts and are generally not interchangeable. For example, a person's age is usually given using Korean numbers, while money is counted using Sino-Korean. Then, in a twist that seems to have been purposely designed to torment you, you learn that sometimes the two number systems are mixed, as when you tell the time, giving the hour in Korean numbers and the minutes in Sino-Korean. If all this sounds confusing, you're not alone.

One of the biggest pitfalls regarding numbers is dealing with numbers larger than five figures. The Korean word for a thousand is *cheon*, but to verbalise the number 10,000 Koreans do not say "sip cheon" ("ten" + "thousand"), but instead introduce a new counting unit, *man* (10,000). Thus, 20,000 is "*i man*". 35,000 is "*sam man, o cheon*" and so on.

So far so good, but the real fun is just beginning. Using *man* as a counting unit for increasingly larger numbers has the effect of shifting the comma so that it appears every four places as opposed to every three (which is where Westerners were trained to put it since elementary school), and can become really confounding as numbers get longer. Four places after *man* is introduced, a new counting unit (*eok*) appears to represent 10 to the eighth power, and four places after that, we meet *jo*, *or* 10 to the twelfth power.

Grasping the idea is not necessarily the hardest part, but learning to process large numbers automatically is something that tends to come slowly or not at all. From my experience, it pays—sometimes literally—to take a moment to double-check large numbers and carefully note the number of places, as it's one of the most common, and sometimes costly, mistakes that even fluent second-language speakers make.

COUNTING UNITS	
1	*il*
10	*sip*
100	*baek*
1,000	*cheon*
10,000	*(il)man*
100,000	*sip man*
1,000,000	*baek man*
10,000,000	*cheon man*
100,000,000	*il eok*
1,000,000,000,000	*il jo*

POLITENESS LEVELS AND HONORIFICS

The cultural imperative to acknowledge status and show respect/deference permeates the Korean language, affecting everything from your choice of pronoun to the way you conjugate verbs, and tends to be one of the toughest aspects of Korean to master. Korean speakers employ different levels of politeness to indicate the relative status of the speaker to both the listener and to the subject of the sentence. Unlike most European languages, Korean verbs are not conjugated with respect to number, person (first second or third) or gender; the forms differ based on whether the listener is of higher status (which requires formal speech, or *jondaetmal*), lower status (which requires informal speech, or *banmal*) or equal status (which employs both depending on the situation). Learning the various forms—and when to use them—takes time, but the good news is that *banmal* is fairly easy to learn once you've gotten the hang of *jondaetmal*, and *jondaetmal* will get you by in the meantime. By relying initially on formal speech, you may occasionally sound funny speaking to toddlers as if they were an esteemed peer, but you effectively eliminate the risk of offending anyone older or more senior than you.

Terms of Address

One of the ways that respect is manifest in everyday speech—and one of the easier aspects of Korean honorifics to quickly get a handle on—is in the practice of addressing people politely. Koreans don't address seniors, strangers or many casual acquaintances by name, but employ an array of titles and honorific suffixes for addressing people directly. A comprehensive rundown of when, whether and how to use them all would almost be the subject of a chapter by itself, but getting a handle on the most common terms isn't hard, and will help you avoid inadvertently throwing shade while you slowly come to grips with the finer points.

The common way to address an older married male is *ajeossi*, and can be used to address taxi drivers, restaurant staff or the guy in the street who has just dropped his wallet. The term used to address older married women is *ajumma*. The term "*imo*"—which indicates the same degree of respect as *ajumma* but conveys warmth—is used for older women with whom one has some familiarity or regular contact, like the proprietor of one of your regular haunts. Neither

Borderline Cases

Many times you will find yourself addressing women whose apparent age makes it hard to decide whether *ajumma* or *agassi* is the more appropriate way to address her. In those borderline cases, it's always safer to err on the side of caution and go with *agassi*. Sometimes I'm correct, and while I've been certainly wrong many times as well, I have yet to be admonished for assuming that a woman was younger than she actually is.

ajumma or *ajeossi* is inappropriate as long as the person is of an age at which most people are likely to be married; it isn't considered inappropriate if the person happens to be single, widowed or divorced. When addressing the elderly, the terms *haraboji* and *halmoni* ("grandfather" and "grandmother", respectively) are used.

Addressing a younger person you don't know is done in a few ways. Boys and girls of school age are addressed as *haksaeng* (student). For a younger woman (like a restaurant server or shop clerk) whose apparent age suggests she is not married, use the term *agassi*. There is no commonly used term to address similarly-aged, unmarried men; they are usually hailed by simply saying "*Jeogiyo!*" (roughly "Hey there!"). *Jeogiyo* is also used to address women in public places when both their younger age and unknown marital status would make both *ajumma* and *agassi* inappropriate.

The term *chingu* (friend) is not a term of direct address, but refers only to people with whom you have an intimate relationship and who are the same age as yourself. Friends or close acquaintances younger than you can be addressed by name, but addressing those older than you requires a specific terms of address.

Addressing Older People

A male addressing an older brother or male friend: *hyoung* or *hyoungnim*
A male addressing an older sister or female friend: *nuna*
A female addressing an older brother or male friend: *oppa*
A female addressing an older sister or female friend: *eonni*

The suffix *-ssi* is attached to a given name to respectfully address familiar people of roughly equal or lower status in a formal or professional setting. Thus I am addressed as John-

ssi when I speak to the administration staff at the university where I teach, and I address them in the same manner.

To show greatest respect, the suffix *-nim* is attached to a person's title. This appears in many common terms of address, like *sonsaengnim* (teacher), *sajangnim* (manager), *wonjangnim* (owner/proprietor), and *hananim* (God). (See Chapter 9: Working in the Country for more detail on addressing people in the workplace).

NEGATIVELY PHRASED QUESTIONS

An odd quirk of the English language is that English speakers can respond to questions like, "Aren't you hungry?" the same way they would respond to, "Are you hungry?" even though you are technically being asked two different questions ("*Are* you, or are you *not*?"). In either case a "yes" indicates that you are hungry, while "no" indicates that you are not, logic be damned.

The Korean language doesn't work like that. To answer negatively phrased questions, Korean speakers directly express either agreement (as in, "Yes, [that is correct; I am not hungry]") or disagreement ("No, [that's incorrect; I *am* hungry]"). So when a Korean asks, "*Bae an gopayo*?" ("Aren't you hungry?"), an answer of "*nae*" (yes) means that you're not hungry, while "*anio*" (no) means that you are.

While the logic of answering in the Korean way is straightforward (and frankly more logical), it still tends to take time to get used to, and can often lead to miscommunication. You can be sure that misunderstandings of this type also work very much the other way around, as Koreans frequently puzzle over how to respond to English questions like, "Isn't my boyfriend handsome?" or "Don't you like my new dress?" without stepping on a landmine. When in doubt, answering in a full sentence instead of a simple yes or no ("He's a dreamboat, and I think your dress is *stunning*!") is a safe bet. Is it not?

MAKING THE EFFORT

Among the many qualities that make people more likely to thrive overseas, perhaps one of the biggest predictors of a rewarding expat experience is the degree to which one makes the effort to learn the local language. Putting in the hours required to gain competence in a language goes far beyond developing communication skills; it is the clearest expression of interest in a people and their culture and thus seldom goes unnoticed or unappreciated. This is especially true in Korea, where the language was systematically devalued and suppressed for decades by a colonial government and is thus an even more palpable object of affection and a source of pride for the Korean people.

Because Korea dwells in the long shadows of its neighbours and has relatively recently emerged as an international cultural presence in its own right, many Koreans you meet will assume that you know little about Korea and don't speak Korean, and will thus often express surprise if you do, or proclaim you a genius for uttering little more than a greeting or a thank you. This sometimes annoys foreigners who have put in the effort to learn, but to be fair, Koreans are often correct in that assumption: for a variety of reasons (difficulty, lack of time, English proficiency of Korean friends) many foreigners in Korea do tend to get little further than a few stock phrases and everyday vocabulary. If you do find yourself receiving a lot of excessive praise, take it in stride; the same underlying assumption will forgive you your mistakes and make people slow to fault you if your Korean doesn't progress much beyond "*Gamsa hamnida*" ("Thank you").

In the 1980s and 1990s foreigners fluent in Korean were so comparatively rare that many of them became minor TV celebrities and radio fixtures. As international interest in Korean language study has grown in recent years, this situation has changed somewhat, though one of the more popular TV programmes today features a talk panel of young foreigners from various countries, which seems to interest people as much for the spectacle of *waegukin* speaking *urimal* at least as much as for the sometimes insightful viewpoints they express.

Even if you are not destined for TV stardom, the slightest competency in Korean language will be not only noticed but appreciated, and the effort to learn is repaid many times over in the form of goodwill from the people you meet, insights into the culture, expanded professional opportunities and personal relationships that might have been difficult or impossible otherwise.

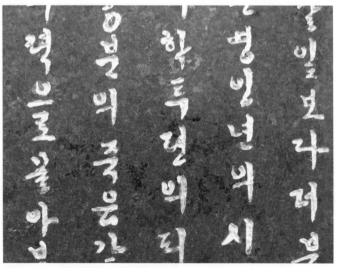

Though normally written from left to right, *Hangeul* is sometimes written in the old top-to-bottom style, as in the case of this memorial inscription.

Unless you are a savant or make a massive commitment to studying, you won't learn to speak Korean like a native, but with some patience and sustained effort, you may however join the growing number of foreigners who achieve fluency—not perfection, but the ability to express oneself freely and easily in a variety of situations—or the many others who attain a level that suffices for day to day life and for enriching your experience in the country. At the lower end of the commitment scale, your "survival Korean" can be up and running in a matter of weeks. Whatever your language-learning goals, be patient, and trust that you will get out of it at least as much as you put into it, and in some cases, a great deal more.

> One of the scholars who originally introduced Hangeul to the Korean people in the Hunminjeongeum Haerye ("Explanations of the Correct Sounds for the Instruction of the People") wrote that, "A wise man can learn it in one morning, and a fool can learn it in ten days." I recall it taking me two or three days to master—feel free to make of that what you will.

HANGEUL

Korean is represented by a phonetic alphabet called *Hangeul*, which is comprised of letters representing vowels and consonants. The letters combine to form clusters (V-C, C-V or C-V-C) that represent one syllable and are read from left to right or top to bottom. These syllables in turn combine in left-to-right strings to form words.

While it's not possible to give a complete rundown of all the nuances and irregularities of Korean pronunciation here, the following can serve as a basic guide to get you on your feet. *Hangeul* was designed to be easy to learn, and every foreigner who has tackled it seems to agree that the creators largely achieved that aim. In a few days (or even hours), you should be happily reading street signs, menus, T-shirts and product labels, just like you did when you first learned your ABCs.

Vowels

Korean has eight simple vowels. The "ㅇ" is an empty (or "null") consonant that is not pronounced and acts as a place holder that vowels must attach to when no other consonant sound is present. They are read from left to right (아, 어, 이, 에, 애) or from top to bottom (오, 우, 으).

Note that the English examples are not precise equivalents; the best way to get a handle on the sounds of Korean is to hear them. You can find good pronunciation guides with audio samples online (See links section).

아	like the "a" in "mama"
어	like the "a" in "ball"
오	like the "o" in "hope"
우	like the "oo" in "too"
으	similar to the "oo" in look, but produced with the base of the tongue further back in the mouth.
이	like "e" in "we"
에*	like "e" in "pet"
애*	like "e" in "pet"

*애 *and* 에 *are virtually indistinguishable in speech, but are important to distinguish in spelling. Mistaking one for the other can result in a different word.*

There are 13 diphthongs, which are vowels blended with either a "y" or "w" sound.

야	like "ya" in "yacht"
애 and 예	like "ye" in "yes"
여	like "ya" in "yawn"
요	like "yo" in "yodel"
유	like "you"
와 (오 + 아)	like "wa" in "wand"
워 (우 + 어)	like "wa" in "warm"
외 (오 + 이)	like "we" in "wet"
위 (우 + 이)	like "wee"
왜 (오 + 애) and 웨 (오 + 에)	like "we" in "wet"
의 (으 + 이)	closer to the "uy" in Spanish "muy" than to any English vowel sound, but formed in the back of the mouth as opposed to by pursing the lips.

Consonants

Hangeul features nine basic consonants, which are listed here with their approximate counterparts in English.

CONSONANT	PRONUNCIATION
ㄱ	g
ㄴ	n
ㄷ	d
ㄹ	r
ㅁ	m
ㅂ	b
ㅅ	s
ㅇ	ng (when it appears as the final sound of a syllable)
ㅈ	j

There are also five aspirated consonants, which are similar to their counterparts above, but are accompanied by a small puff of air.

ㅊ	like "ch" in "chin"
ㅋ	like "k" in "kite"
ㅌ	like "t" in "too"
ㅍ	like "p" in "pat"
ㅎ	like "h" in "hat"

Some of the consonants also form double consonants (ㅃ, ㅉ, ㄸ, ㄲ, ㅆ). These are pronounced with the mouth held more tensely than the basic consonant, and with no aspiration.

ㅃ	like "p" in "speck"
ㅉ	like "dg" in "gadget"
ㄸ	like "t" in "stack"
ㄲ	like "k" in "skit"
ㅆ	like "s" in "sing"

Consonants can combine with a vowel or a vowel and another consonant. They take the place of the null consonant ("ㅇ") when they appear at the beginning of a syllable, and may also appear at the bottom of a letter cluster when they appear at the end of a syllable.

고 – "go"	곰 – "gom"
나 – "na"	날 – "nal"
두 – "doo"	둑 – "dook"
지 – "ji"	집 – "jip"

String syllables together to make multi-syllable words.

김치	kimchi
태권도	taekwondo
바나나	banana

NON-VERBAL COMMUNICATION

The "Embarrassed Laugh"

Laughter is a human universal, but while all humans express amusement by laughing, not all laughter means that the person laughing is amused. In fact, research tells us that most laughter occurs for reasons other than humour: Some laughter serves a social purpose, like signaling agreement or making ourselves more likeable; some laughs are sarcastic or even sinister; and sometimes we laugh merely because someone else is laughing. We also laugh as a defense against nervousness or stress, and may find ourselves laughing at seemingly inappropriate times. In a similar vein, Koreans sometimes laugh or giggle in situations when they are embarrassed, a response which is often misunderstood and is occasionally the cause of friction and bad feelings when it involves a foreigner. Though it may take some getting used to, you're better off learning to trust that the server who has just spilled coffee on you is laughing because he is mortified, not because he finds the stain on your pants hilarious.

Forearms crossed in front of the body to form an "X" indicate a big and unequivocal "no". Depending on the situation, this can be employed to mean anything from "No smoking" to "I'm sorry, sir, but we don't have that in XXL."

The two-finger peace sign (palm facing outward) can often be seen when people pose for photographs. It doesn't appear to mean anything; it's just kind of a thing.

Make two fists and extend both index fingers, place your fists on both sides of your head with your index fingers pointing up, so that they resemble the horns of a bull. This is the Korean sign for "angry". Note that it isn't normally done by the angry person, but by someone who wants to warn you that someone else is angry.

A fist with the thumb protruding between the middle and ring fingers is Korean shorthand for sexual intercourse. This is good to keep in mind if you enjoy amusing toddlers with the "I Stole Your Nose" game.

KONGLISH

Konglish is a general term for Korean words that derive in some way from English, either as a direct loan word, an abbreviation or compound coined from English parts, or the result of a new meaning applied to a familiar word. The borrowing process is dynamic and ongoing with new coinages appearing all the time, but the following is a sampling of the more lasting creations that you're likely to hear.

When a waiter brings you a cola you haven't ordered and tells you it is **service**, he is telling you that it is "complimentary" or "on the house".

M.T. ("membership training") are short excursions that student groups take for the purpose of bonding. *M.T.*s are especially common among first-year university students.

If you are asked to name your favourite **talent**, the speaker wants to know your favourite "TV celebrity", not that you know how to tap dance, balance a hockey stick on your forehead or whip up a mean soufflé.

Eye shopping is how Koreans refer to "window shopping", not the thing that pirates do on their days off.

Skinship is the word Koreans use to describe non-sexual physical contact, like holding hands, wrapping your arm around someone's waist or draping it across their shoulders. *Skinship* is a favourite among foreigners in informal polls of Konglish coinages that should be officially adopted into English.

If a hospitalised Korean friend tells you he has been fitted with a *gips* and has been put on a *ringel*, don't panic; he is telling you that he has gotten a "cast" for a broken bone, and is hooked up to an "IV drip".

The exclamation *Fighting* is a cheer of encouragement, similar to "Go, team!" or "You can do it!"

A Swiss army knife is called a *MacGuyver knife*, after the absurdly handy main character of the late 1980s TV series. Useful for camping, fishing and making catapults out of sticks, twine, and Rosary beads.

In Korea, a dress shirt is called a *Y-shirt*. *Y*? I don't know.

Hunting in Korea does not involve hounds, high-powered rifles or Day-glo vests, but refers to trying to "pick up," "hook up," "pull," or otherwise find a romantic partner for the evening. An alternative is to go to a club and try *booking*, which is the practice of having the club staff introduce a potential partner and letting you take it from there. *Fighting!*

ROMANISATION

As most of the sounds of Korean roughly correspond to the sounds of English, one would expect the rendering of Korean words in the Roman alphabet to be a fairly straightforward matter.

It is, and it isn't. For a long time, a system of romanisation called the McCune-Reischauer system was the official system, but it was burdened by an inventory of diacritics for vowels with no close analogue, apostrophes to denote aspired consonants and hyphens which often ended up being omitted, leading to ambiguity and multiple spellings of the same word.

To cut down on the confusion, the Korean government issued a revised system of romanisation in 2000 to be the official system for place names, thoroughfares, maps, names and such. The new system represents an improvement in this author's opinion, but it isn't perfect; after all, it is an attempt to transliterate a language into a writing system that was not designed for it. The trouble spots are the ones you might expect: the sounds that are most unlike English, which for those who are unfamiliar with their romanisation, can be confusing. Most vowels and consonants have a romanised spelling that generally leads to a close-enough rendering of the original sounds; the ones that seem to cause the most trouble are the following:

LETTER	ROMANISED SPELLING
어	eo
여	yeo
으	eu
의	ui
외	oe

Because these combinations also appear in English but

with different pronunciations (e.g. **yeo**man, fr**ui**t, rod**eo**, etc), it takes a little bit of reorienting to read them as Korean sounds, and to remember for example that "*hoe*" in a Korean context is not pronounced like the garden implement, but by something closer to "hweh" (and refers to what English speakers call "sashimi").

The new romanisation system has been widely adopted, but you should note that it isn't uniformly applied on the personal level, particularly when people romanise their own names. For example, Rhee, Yi and Lee are all variant spellings of the same name, as are Kim and Gim, Park and Bak, and many others that can leave you wondering if one is referring to the same family. While there isn't much the government can do about how people write their names, place names are now standardised, and many long-timers in Korea remember 2000 as the year that Pusan became Busan, Taegu became Daegu, Kwangju became Gwangju, and so on.

STUDYING KOREAN

Depending on your budget, time and learning goals, there are a variety of ways to go about learning Korean.

KIIP – Korea Immigration and Integration Program is a free programme run through the Korean Ministry of Justice in cooperation with Hankuk University of Foreign Studies to help immigrants integrate into Korean society and earn points toward citizenship, though it is open to anyone who is a legal resident of Korea under any visa status. To take the class, go to www.socinet.go.kr and register for a pre-test at a testing centre near you.

Yonsei University's Korean Language Institute (www.yskli.com) offers one of the largest and best known programmes in Korea, geared toward students pursuing further university education in Korea, but is open to anyone.

Lexis Korea – Located in Gangnam, Seoul, the Lexis Korea language programme gets high marks for flexibility, as it allows professionals to fit Korean classes into their work schedules.

Gangnam UC-Riverside – GNUCR (www.gnucr.org) is partnered with Seoul National University, and offers the same programme. Evenings classes and proximity to the business district make this programme popular with professionals.

Many universities in cities around Korea offer Korean language programmes. Inquire locally or online about universities in your area to find out more.

Online Resources

Talk to Me in Korean comes highly recommended by many users. They have a website (www.talktomeinkorean.com) and a YouTube channel with frequent lessons on everyday Korean that are suitable for beginner through intermediate learners. They offer lots of audio and video, and grammar explanations in plain English.

The King Sejong Institute website (www.sejonghakdang.org) has lectures online and materials for download.

Rocket languages.com offers free resources for practicing pronunciation.

Koreanclass101.com is free to register, and gives you access to podcasts and associated phone apps with short lessons on beginner Korean.

The University of California, Berkeley has a free online college-level Korean course appropriate for high beginner to intermediate learners at www.language.berkeley.edu/korean.

Zkorean.com is a good place to go for pronunciation help, and features a bank of audio samples to help you get a feel for the sounds of Korean.

CHAPTER 9

WORKING IN THE COUNTRY

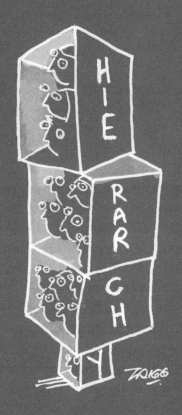

In Korea, business is personal.

— Daniel Tudor,
Korea: The Impossible Country

THE WORKPLACE ENVIRONMENT

TRADITION   THE FUTURE

The Korean workplace is a reflection of Korean society in general, in that it adheres to many aspects of tradition, while simultaneously keeping one eye on the future, trying to strike a balance that allows it to compete in the ever-evolving global economy. As one might expect, a heavy Confucian influence permeates the Korean workplace: a preference for hierarchy and formality; respect for age, position or rank; valuing education and testing as a means of advancement; and a conformist ethos as opposed to encouraging the standout individual.

True to the Confucian imperative to know one's place in society, Korean companies, schools and government

agencies have a clearly defined pecking order with many tiers and titles, each accompanied by entitlements and responsibilities between senior and junior. Those occupying the lower station are expected to show deference and loyalty to those above, while the higher-ups strive to be paternalistic, in the positive sense of the word. While demanding the kind of obedience that a father would expect of his children, the Korean boss also has a responsibility to be benevolent, and to make employees feel valued by the organisation. Many companies thus give gifts to their employees on milestone occasions like birthdays, weddings, the birth of a child or the death of a family member. Some companies even arrange dates for single employees to assist them in the search for a suitable marriage partner. *Hwaeshik* (staff dinners) involve lots of food and drink, and are aimed at inculcating an affinity for the group, ideally to a point where the interests of the individual and the company coincide.

Loyalty

Many observers have likened the Korean company to a family, in which those at the bottom exchange their loyalty and deference for a sense of belonging and security. This is still true in large part, but one must be careful about overstating the "family" aspect of the Korean workplace. Older employees have long been forced into early retirement, both because they cost more to retain, and to avoid the risk of awkward situations where an older subordinate must answer to a younger boss. After the so-called "IMF crisis" of 1997-1998, many Korean companies laid off workers—something that was unthinkable only a few years before—and began the process of preferring cheaper contract workers to full-time salaried employees with full benefits. Today, something like one-third of Korean workers work under such terms, which has had the predictable effect of dampening employee loyalty and creating a greater willingness to jump ship if something better comes along.

The Confucian legacy has also produced a male-dominated workforce, and the gap widens the further up the ladder one looks. Large companies have long been reluctant to promote women for fear of having them quit after getting married and having a child, and because maternity leave was too short to be effective. While this is still largely true, it too is showing tentative signs of change. As low birth rates combine with longer life expectancy to create a rapidly greying society, Korea needs women to fill the gap or risk putting a terminal strain on pension reserves. Many foreign companies in Korea have been snapping up talented women, and it's becoming harder for Korean companies to overlook them as the benefits of tapping into a talented and vastly undervalued human resource become obvious.

The gender gap remains wide, and progress is admittedly slow, but it is inching in the right direction, as the inclusion of women in the professional ranks has become a matter not only of efficiency or egalitarian impulses, but of national competitiveness and survival.

Many other cracks in the old order are also beginning to show. At some younger companies (like tech start-ups), skills, creativity and vision are what count, as opposed to length of service, and it's become common at such companies to see the boardrooms populated by people in their 30s and 40s. Even big players like Samsung feel the need for change, as increased competition is pushing them to realign their corporate structures to be less autocratic and more streamlined, and to provide both the organisational and cultural space for talented up-and-comers to up and come.

In June 2016, Samsung announced that it was undertaking a major initiative to make the corporate giant function more like a small, flexible company. "Startup Samsung", as the initiative was dubbed by the directors, aims to rid the company of its rigid hierarchy and make the company more competitive in a global economy that requires flexibility, efficiency and innovation.

The proposed reforms, to be implemented in March 2017, are nothing less than profound: To minimise the stifling sense of hierarchy, they plan to reduce the number of management levels from seven tiers to four, and will try to eliminate the use of titles by having workers address each other with the generic honorific marker "-*nim*" or use English names. To streamline communication, they will allow people working in the field to report directly to levels as high as vice president, and they announced as-yet-unspecified plans to make promotion more meritocratic, as opposed to the current system based on length of service. To enhance efficiency and productivity, meetings will be limited to one hour, and if all this were not sweeping enough, they also plan to permit workers to wear shorts in the sweltering Seoul summers, take longer vacations and leave the office at a more humane and reasonable hour.

To be sure, these changes will not happen overnight nor be perfectly applied, but this writer is not betting against some form of radical changes taking place. South Korea in general, and Samsung in particular, have shown a remarkable ability to be pragmatic and flexible when the chips are down and survival is at stake. After all, nobody would have dreamed that a company whose main business once upon a time was exporting dried fish would one day lead the world in cutting-edge memory chips, TVs and smartphones. Stay tuned.

Korean businesses and schools evidence much the same emphasis on hard work and industry that built the Korea of today from the ashes of war, and workers come under considerable social pressure to keep their noses to the grindstone, even when legally entitled to take time off. Koreans work among the longest hours of any OECD nation (second to Mexico), and sometimes spend nights and weekends at the office, despite the establishment of a 5-day work week in 2004. A Korean worker has to be very sick indeed before he or she will take a sick day; a more common sight is to see them come in wearing a surgical mask, and spend the day resting feverish heads on a desk. A recent news article told of a man who requested to take a short (and legally-guaranteed) paternal leave after the birth of his first child. His boss responded by asking him whether he was the one who had given birth, effectively answering his question.

Social relationships are paramount in Korea, and perhaps nowhere is the high Korean valuation of personal connections more apparent than in the world of business. Koreans feel strong bonds with people from the same hometown, with graduates of their alma mater or with people with whom they served in the military. While this is true to some extent everywhere, in Korea those bonds are unusually pronounced, one often finds people going far out of their way to maintain a relationship, placate a school chum or perform a favour for an old pal from boot camp. Many business decisions reflect the primacy of these bonds, and though it may seem contrary to what appears to Western observers to be in their interest, to a Korean, prioritising those relationships is common sense.

Foreigners who work in Korea are quick to notice that strict empirical logic doesn't always hold sway in their new surroundings, but tend to be slower in grasping that many of the things we take as universal business values are not always valued to the same degree in other cultures, but are instead dependent on the particular priorities and assumptions of our own cultural mindsets. While things like "maximising shareholder value", "constructive feedback" and "lowering costs" seem to Westerners to have the same inviolability as the laws of gravity or holy writ, in Korea those imperatives can sometimes take a backseat to what Koreans consider to be higher values: helping a friend, saving face (whether their own or someone else's) or the general humanistic considerations that are embodied in the Korean concept of *injeong* (humanity). This is not to say that Koreans are uniquely incapable of doing things that don't make sense, or that one must approve of the behaviour that results from differing cultural priorities. It is good, however, to be aware that competing priorities exist when evaluating the behaviour that flows from them.

Despite the formality of many Korean organisations, there is also an observable tendency to be flexible with rules and regulations, and to not follow protocol to the letter when it suits the situation. Actual slackers and cheats aside, even the most virtuous Koreans feel less bound by decree, regulation and even law than by what their adherence to *injeong* sometimes dictates. Instead of asking whether a course of action is in strict accordance with regulations, they may be more likely to weigh it in terms of whether it is the right thing to do and to act accordingly.

WORKPLACE ETIQUETTE

The same basic ideas for interacting with Koreans in general apply to the workplace, though there are a few points more relevant to the workplace to keep in mind.

Introductions

In general, it's better to be introduced to someone rather than to introduce yourself. It's not to say that it isn't done, but people generally respond better to someone who has been vouched for by a trusted third person. The Western style of approaching someone and introducing yourself can be met with mixed results.

When meeting someone for the first time, it's customary to shake hands and bow simultaneously. When you are introduced to someone of roughly the same status, offer your right hand and bow slightly (say 15 degrees) at the waist, and bow slightly deeper for people much more senior than you. Also be aware that the firm handshake is not a thing in Korea; Korean handshakes are often little more than a very cursory contact, so it's best not to go around crunching people's metacarpals and making character assessments if the grip isn't up to your old standards.

Likewise, don't read too much into a lack of eye contact, which does not carry the same connotations of honesty that it has in some Western countries. Too much eye contact is considered rude in Korea, and you will often see the junior partner in any social relationship gazing downward when speaking with a senior. This is a sign of deference and should not be taken as a sign of disrespect or untrustworthiness.

Another universal feature of meeting a Korean for the first time is the exchange of business cards. Carry a good supply and be prepared to receive many in return. When having cards printed, many people opt to have one side in English and the other in Korean. It should also carry your title, as this is one of the most salient facts about you that Koreans will want to know after your name.

When offering a business card, do so with the card in your right hand, and your left hand supporting the right arm beneath the elbow. Likewise, it's best to receive a business card with two hands, and examine it for a moment before filing it away. Quickly stashing a card without looking at it can be taken as a slight. Show interest.

Addressing People

In a hierarchical society like Korea, one's title is a key component of social status and personal identity. In the workplace, Koreans address those more senior than themselves by using the person's last name, plus their title, plus the honorific marker -*nim*. Thus, a *sajang* (manager) named Kim Jae-gyun is addressed as "Kim *sajangnim*". Using the title and honorific marker without the surname is also acceptable. There are a variety of titles, some you will encounter more frequently than others; the best policy is to know the titles of those more senior than you, and to use them whenever addressing them directly or speaking about them to Korean colleagues.

Note that it is *never* acceptable to address someone older or more senior than you by his or her first name. The chummy informality of the British or American workplace is a world apart from the Korean office, where addressing our hypothetical manager as "Jae-gyun" is possibly the quickest and surest way to irretrievably offend him.

For those who are working in primary schools and *hagwons*, similar rules hold. First names are acceptable only for students and friends your age or younger. Your teaching colleagues are addressed as *sonsaengnim* ("teacher" + honorific marker), and the school principal as *gyojang seonsaengnim*. At the university level, Korean professors are addressed as *gyosunim*, and deans as *hakjangnim*.

Some Koreans, especially those with hard to pronounce names, have taken to adopting English names to make things easier for their foreign colleagues and contacts. In such cases it's acceptable to call the person by the name they ask to be called, though it's still a good idea to know his or her Korean name, because chances are that their Korean colleagues will not know them by their foreign name, which can complicate efforts to track them down or pass along messages. Note that the same effort to have Korean work colleagues call you by your first name may just as often result in your being known forever after as "Mr John".

Saving Face

When disagreements arise, rather than decrying something as "wrong", you can try couching it in a more self-effacing, Korean way (e.g., "My understanding is different") or respectfully expressing your objections in a private one-on-one setting. Learning to pick one's battles is also a vital skill. You don't need to kowtow or throw all good sense out the window in order to get along, but merely to show the appropriate deference that someone of a certain position has a right to expect in the Korean context, and to resolve differences in a way that maintains the general harmony and preserves the relationship.

Another way to avoid damaging someone's face is to avoid going over people's heads. The Western practice of going straight to the top guy more often backfires in Korea, where a decision-making process may involve several levels of bureaucracy before it reaches the top for approval. Attempting to cut middle people out of the process can alienate them, and can be a quick way of ensuring that the relationship sours.

Showing anger is likewise a no-no. Whatever the situation, keeping a cool head is the best way to have a shot at resolution. Blowing up at people may sometimes get short-term results, but can have damaging social repercussions.

While visiting a hospital for his annual physical exam, a newly-hired university instructor was told that his insurance didn't cover his young child, whom he had brought for a check-up as well. Having been previously assured otherwise by university administration, he proceeded to argue his point with a flustered young nurse at an escalating volume in front of everyone assembled, causing such a scene that word of the incident filtered back to the university along with the call for clarification. When he was not re-upped at the end of his contract, it was widely and immediately understood that the first and last nails in the coffin had all been driven home in that one, hot-headed encounter.

Eating and Drinking

Whether it's a cafeteria lunch with colleagues or a formal company dinner, eating and drinking is a central part of work culture in Korea, as it represents one of the most fundamental ways of building the human side of a professional relationship. In general, the etiquette involved mirrors that in Chapter 6, but with a few extra points to keep in mind.

One of the ways that Korean companies cultivate loyalty and forge interpersonal bonds is through the *hwaesik*, or staff dinner, which can be as often as a couple of times a week, or as seldom as once a year. For many foreigners and Koreans alike, the *hwaesik* can be a burden, especially when they are frequent or the boss likes to tie one on. For others, it's a welcome break from formality and routine, a chance to forge and maintain social relationships with colleagues or business contacts or just an occasional good feed on the company dime. However you feel about them, if you are invited to one, it's best to consider it obligatory. Regularly bowing out for no good reason sends a signal that you're not a team player or are trying to claim special privilege, and may earn you mistrust from your seniors, and the resentment of your colleagues, many of whom would just as gladly skip it as well.

At dinner, be mindful of the seating arrangements. Senior members have a place of honour either at the head or centre of the table, so if you are not sure if you are about to sit in the wrong place, wait for someone to seat you. *Hwaesiks* usually begin with a speech by the most senior member of the party. Don't begin eating before he or she does.

Many large *hwaesiks* are held these days at buffet-style restaurants, where even the pickiest eater can manage to find something to fill up on, though with smaller groups you may be taken to other types of restaurants (pork or beef barbecue being perhaps the most common). Many popular Korean foods go down equally well with Westerners, though there will inevitably be some dishes that require you to draw on your sense of adventure. You don't have to pretend to like everything offered to you, but it is polite to at least try it once, particularly if it's a special dish that your hosts have gone out of their way to procure. Many Koreans tend to assume that Korean food is too strange or too spicy to foreigners (though they also tend to overrate the strangeness and the spiciness), so they will not be offended if you decline subsequent servings. At worst, you chase it with some beer and move on, and if you do like it, you've just added one more source of joy to your life.

Korean company dinners always involve a greater or lesser quantity of alcohol (see Chapter 6 for a full discussion of drinking customs), and may move beyond dinner to include one or several more rounds at various other locations. No matter how you feel about singing, if you end up at a *noraebang*, you will be expected to belt out a song or two. If you're a good singer, you'll win some admirers, and if you're a bad singer, you'll score points for being unafraid to let your colleagues see you butcher a song, while sending a strong signal of your willingness to bond with the group.

GIFT GIVING

When doing business in Korea, gifts are commonly exchanged when meeting for the first time. The gift need not be extravagant, but should be of roughly equal value and should be gift-wrapped. Korean shops sell all manners of gift sets for all occasions, or something special from your home country (like a bottle of scotch) will go over just as well or better. It is considered polite to refuse a gift once or twice before accepting. After the obligatory refusal, receive the gift with two hands.

Koreans also give gifts on major holidays to staff, clients and business partners. In the run-up to Chuseok and Seollal, supermarket aisles and department stores are stacked full of gift sets containing anything from wine to ginseng to Spam. Many Koreans will not expect you to observe this custom, so consider it a golden opportunity

The Kim Young-ran Law

For a long time, there has been a blurry line between gift-giving and bribery in Korea, and many have abused the custom of expressing thanks or friendship in order to curry favour by lavishing public officials with expensive dinners, golf outings, or envelopes full of cash. In an effort to cut down on this, the Korean government passed The Anti-Corruption and Bribery-Prohibition Act (aka "The Kim Young-ran Law", after the judge who proposed it), which went into effect in September 2016. The law applies to gifts given to civil servants, teachers and journalists, and places strict limits on the amounts that may be spent on gifts (50,000 won), meals (30,000 won) and the amount of cash given as wedding gifts (100,000 won).

Though some complained that this would hurt the economy or dampen what is in essence an important means of expressing gratitude or friendship, many hailed the law as a long-overdue step toward levelling of the playing field and encouraging greater transparency and public integrity. Whether the new law proves to be effective remains to be seen.

to score major points with your Korean associates, employees and clients.

PATIENCE AND HUMILITY

Patience is an asset when conducting business in Korea. Though Korean organisations are hierarchical, decisions tend not to flow from the top down but are more of a multi-level consensus-building process, and thus take time to coalesce. Though this seems counter-intuitive to many Westerners' assumptions about how a Confucian-influenced system is supposed to function, the reality is that pushing for a prompt decision or going straight to the head honcho will be ineffective at best, and can at worst be counter-productive. Be patient, and take solace in the thought that though the decision-making process may be slower than what you are used to, implementation tends to be swift.

One of the costs of swift implementation is the short-notice deadline, another fact of life in Korea that will occasionally put your patience to the test. Information trickles through Korean organisations on a need-to-know basis, and many Koreans and expats alike at some point find themselves needing to know something some time before they happened to find out about it. Learn to roll with it, and do your best to get plugged in to as many sources of information as you can to minimise the impact of surprise directives.

An attitude of humility also goes a long way. Talking up your company, product, skills, or achievements may come off as prideful or self-aggrandising. It's also good to bear this tendency in mind when evaluating the statements of Korean contacts, particularly on resumes or CVs, which are sometimes so humble as to cross over to self-deprecation.

DOS AND DON'TS

Do...

Communicate clearly. When speaking English, tailor your speech to your audience. Speak a bit slower and with clearer diction than you normally do. Repeat key points and give them a moment to sink in. If you are planning to attend a meeting, some recommend sending written materials prior to the meeting to give your counterparts time to prepare and digest some of the content beforehand. If possible, use visuals and give some time to let information be processed.

Choose your words for maximum clarity, not to impress. Chances are that the jargon of your particular field is understood, but in general it's good to prefer higher-frequency vocabulary than the types of words one finds in the *New York Times* crossword puzzle. Pay attention to the terms your interlocutor uses and understands, and use those. Also try to avoid idiomatic language, and whenever possible prefer a single verb to a phrasal verb or idiom, as these are usually the last things a second language speaker learns, if ever. Thus, sales are not "picking up"; they are "increasing". Facilities aren't "up to snuff", but "satisfactory". Site inspections weren't "held up"; they were "delayed". You get the drift (or rather, you "understand").

It's good not to automatically assume that "yes" means anything more than "I have just heard the sounds that came out of your mouth." Affirmative replies do not necessarily signal agreement or even understanding, as many Koreans would rather eat glass than admit that they have failed to understand something that was said in English. Though such responses can be vexing, they often do it to save face; both theirs (by not admitting a lack of English fluency, which may be tied to their standing in the company) and yours (by not implying that you have presented information in a manner that was confusing). If you sense that something has not gotten through or needs clarification, it's better to discuss it on the sidelines to give your counterpart a chance to ask questions privately without risking embarrassment.

For similar reasons, Koreans will often not say "no" directly and unequivocally, and often prefer to soften the blow by saying things like, "It will be hard to do that," or, "That may be possible." If repeated inquiries keep producing this kind of reply, or the "hard" or "possible" thing keeps getting put off, it could very well be an indirect way of saying "no".

Take meetings seriously. Apart from the difficulty of making jokes land across cultural and linguistic barriers, this can sometimes be taken as a lack of gravity or as disrespect for the proceedings. It's not that Koreans lack a sense of humour; they just don't consider work meetings the time for expressing it.

Be sensitive to the nationalist sentiments of Korean people. Koreans are aware of the problems in their society, and many of your Korean colleagues will be happy to enumerate them for you; but like most people, they often bristle at hearing them pointed out by strangers. Be wary of being publicly critical of Korea, and if you do feel it necessary to air a critique, couching your criticism in an acknowledgement of other good points would be a good way to do it. This attitude also extends to Korean food, which is near and dear to the hearts of the Korean people. You don't have to like it, but bashing it to your Korean colleagues won't win you any friends.

There's no harm in being proud of your home country or in showing it, but going on about it at length may come across as lacking in humility or as an implicit swipe at the way things are done in Korea. Also be aware that because of South Korea's turbulent history with its neighbour to the east, unflattering comparisons between Korea and Japan are made at your peril.

Acquire a reputation as the "Yes" person. Apart from not saying "no" directly, it's helpful not to too often say no even indirectly, especially in the beginning of your sojourn. This is not to say you should not place reasonable limits on your willingness to help, or that you should let people walk all over you, but that helping people, even when there is no immediate short-term benefit to yourself, demonstrates loyalty and is one way of acquiring a reputation as a team player. Being known as a dependable person is important everywhere; in Korea it shows that you are willing to make the small sacrifices that many Koreans shoulder daily, and increases your chances of being the name at the top of the list when an opportunity arises down the road. Try to look past short-term benefit or immediate quid pro quo calculations and trust that Koreans place a high premium on loyalty and commitment, and tend to repay it in time.

Also remember that loyalty, once established, is not a one-way street. Koreans go to great lengths to help those with whom they have an established and sincere relationship, even when it is inconvenient for them to do so.

Take time to develop personal relationships. The importance of personal relationships in Korean organisations is difficult to overstate. Personal connections are an important part of doing business anywhere, but according to Peter Underwood, a market analyst and lifelong Seoul resident, making an "emotional connection" is perhaps even more important in Korea. "Work on relationships," he advises would-be entrants to the world of Korean business, "Just as you study your discipline to stay on the cutting edge of your particular industry, in Korea, you need to invest in relationships, build relationships, maintain relationships. You have to pro-actively do that."

Before any serious business can begin, a relationship must be established, and would-be business partners need to show that they are trustworthy and committed. Cutting to the chase may work against you, as Koreans will often prefer to take more time than Westerners are accustomed to in laying the preliminary personal foundations before getting down to brass tacks.

Koreans build these relationships in several ways, probably chief of which is going out for dinner, drinks and further entertainment. When visiting someone at their office, always accept their offer of coffee or tea, even if you don't drink it. Eschewing even such small opportunities to forge a personal connection can send a bad signal.

Beyond the work environment, forging relationships with Koreans is key to escaping the Korea of strangers and creating the conditions for experiencing the best that Korea has to offer: the genuine warmth, generosity, and consideration of friends and acquaintances.

Double-check the numbers (especially large ones). Dealing with large numbers is a common source of confusion and mistranslation (See Chapter 8: Learning the Language). If something seems not to add up, write it down and count the decimal places to clarify, and don't assume that someone is necessarily trying to put one over on you.

Carry business cards at all times, and **receive them properly** from others.

Be punctual, and be prepared to tolerate a certain degree of tardiness. The old notion of working on "Korean time" has disappeared: Korean professionals are generally punctual and expect the same of others, though crammed schedules and snarled traffic can often lead to tardiness. Be tolerant in such cases—it may be you one day—and phone ahead if you anticipate being late. Likewise, when Koreans are running late, they will generally let you know.

Show commitment to your company, school or organisation. If you intend to stay in Korea for a while, lay a good foundation by showing that you are a committed team player. Bowing out of company outings, dinners, meetings and seminars shows people that you are not willing to be a part of the group, and can adversely affect your standing in the organisation. Bear in mind that most of your Korean colleagues will also quietly chafe at having to go through the motions of these events as well, and tend to look down on people who skip out.

Dress the part. Whether you are a CEO or a kindergarten teacher, dressing with the formality appropriate to your role is important. Koreans in all occupations tend to be formal—even taxi drivers wear uniforms. Take your cues from your Korean colleagues. Dressing down consistently sends subtle but noticeable signals to those around you, and fairly or not, these will add up and be factored into their impression of your seriousness, professionalism, commitment and willingness to conform to expectations.

Beyond the groups related to your company, school, or organization, other groups to consider joining are:
· Chambers of Commerce
· Lions Club, Rotary International, Kiwanis, and other service organizations
· KOTESOL (Korea Teachers of English to Speakers of Other Languages)

Be a joiner. It's often worth the effort to get involved in things like company hiking groups, soccer clubs and professional associations. Getting involved demonstrates commitment, can be a valuable source of information and scuttlebutt and can further forge the bonds of familiarity, friendship and trust with your personal and professional networks.

Don't...

… address older or more senior colleagues or business associates by their first name. Know their title, and use it with the *–nim* suffix.

… conduct business on the phone. Phone calls are for scheduling meetings, not for having them. Business should be discussed face to face.

… assume that your own business values are universal and are prioritised in the same way.

… use your index finger to point at someone. When it's necessary to point someone out, use the whole hand with palm facing upward.

CHAPTER 10

FAST FACTS

‘After difficulty comes delight.’

— Korean proverb

Official Name
The Republic of Korea (*Daehan Minguk* in Korean)

Capital
Seoul

Flag
The Korean flag is called the *taegeukgi*, and is composed of a red and blue yin/yang symbol in the center of a white field, which is flanked at the corners by solid and broken black bars in four sets of three bars each.

Time
GMT +9

Telephone Country Code
+82

Land Area
98,477 sqm

Climate
With the exception of Jejudo, whose climate is borderline sub-tropical, South Korea has a temperate climate and four seasons. Summers are hot and humid, with monsoon rains in June and July. Winters range from cold and snowy up north to mild in the southern provinces, where heavy snowfall is

rare. Spring and fall are quite pleasant and are a good time to be outdoors.

Population
50.8 million (April 2016 estimate by the National Statistical Office)

Religion
South Korea is a religiously plural society. 29% of Koreans claim Christian affiliation (which breaks down to 18% Protestant and 11% Catholic), about 23% of Koreans claim Buddhist affiliation, and 46.5% of South Koreans claim no religious affiliation. Millions of Koreans also practice shamanistic folk traditions to varying degrees, but because there is no central church or unifying dogma, and because such traditions often overlap with other faiths, it is not considered a formal religious affiliation and their precise numbers aren't known.

Government Structure
South Korea is a republic with three branches of government. The executive branch is headed by a president who serves one five-year term; the 300-member National Assembly comprises the legislative branch; and the judicial branch is composed of a Supreme Court and a Constitutional Court.

Currency
South Korean won

Industries
South Korea's largest industries are electronics manufacturing, shipbuilding, telecommunications, steel, automobile manufacturing, and chemicals.

Exports

Korea exports several high end products, like semiconductors, automobiles, ships, telecommunications equipment, and LCDs.

Ethnic Groups

With a population that is about 96% Korean, South Korea is one of the most ethnically homogenous countries in the world. The remaining 4% hail mainly from China, South and Southeast Asia, and several Western countries.

Airports

Incheon International Airport is South Korea's main international air hub. Limited international connections are also available at Gimhae Airport (Busan), Gimpo Airport (Seoul), Jeju International airport, and others.

Electricity

220v, 60hz

FAMOUS KOREANS

Politics

Park Geun-hye is the daughter of former president Park Chung-hee, and in 2012, she was elected as South Korea's first female president. In 2016, Park was embroiled in an influence-peddling and bribery scandal involving an unofficial aide, **Choi Soon-shil**, and she was impeached in December 2016 (the impeachment was upheld by the Constitutional Court and formalised in March 2017). Park was arrested on 30 March on thirteen charges related to the scandal, and she remains in custody at this writing while her trial plays out.

Moon Jae-in is the current president of South Korea. A lawyer and former chief of staff to President **Roh Moo-hyun**, Moon ran for the presidency in 2012 as the Minjoo Party candidate, but was defeated by Park Geun-hye. Following Park's impeachment in March 2017, the presidential election was moved up from 20 December to 9 May. Moon won by a plurality of votes, and was inaugurated the following day.

Ahn Chul-soo is a physician, software developer, and member of the Korean National Assembly since 2013. Ahn made his first foray into politics the year before, when he entered the 2012 presidential race, only to withdraw one month before the election to support Moon Jae-in. In 2017, Ahn again threw his hat into the ring as the People's Party candidate, but polled third behind Moon and Hong Jun-pyo of the Liberty Korea Party. As the founder of the People's Party, Ahn remains a fixture on the national political scene.

Chun Doo-hwan became the president of Korea after seizing power in a 1979 coup following the assassination of President Park Chung-hee. As president, Chun was deeply unpopular, and his administration saw many large-scale protests. In 1996, Chun was tried, convicted, and sentenced to death for his role in the 1980 "Gwangju Uprising", in which many civilians were killed by soldiers sent to retake the city, though he was later pardoned by president **Kim Young-sam**. Chun now lives in a walled compound in Seoul, and in March 2017, he published a memoir in which he denies responsibility for the massacre, a claim that was met with outrage and derision by relatives of the victims.

Lee Myung-bak is a businessman and former Seoul mayor who served as South Korea's president from 2008 to 2013. As Seoul mayor (2002-2006) he was known for spearheading many large civic projects, like the creation of Seoul Plaza, Seoul Forest Park and the popular Cheonggyecheon stream revitalisation project. As president, he didn't quite enjoy the same success in realising his plan for a Grand Korean Waterway (a system of canals and rivers linking Seoul and Busan) and his "7-4-7 plan", which aimed for seven per cent growth, a $40,000 per capita income and Korea becoming the world's seventh largest economy.

Park Won-soon is the current mayor of Seoul, a post which he initially won in 2011 and for which he was re-elected in 2014. A lawyer and former human rights activist, Park often ran afoul of the Park Chung-hee administration in the 1970s for protesting Park's increasingly authoritarian policies.

Entertainment

Park Bo-gum is an award-winning actor who has appeared in many popular TV series including *Hello Monster* and *Love in the Moonlight* (2016), as well as several popular films, including 2014's *The Admiral: Roaring Currents* and *Coin Locker Girl* (2015).

Song Joong-ki was an original cast member of the popular TV variety show *Running Man*, and has since starred in several movie and TV roles, including a lead role in the series *Descendants of the Sun*, which had many fans across Asia and established him as a major Hallyu star.

Kim Ki-duk is an award-winning film director, whose work has won accolades in festivals from Venice to Cannes. His 2003 film *Spring, Summer, Fall, Winter…and Spring* was named by influential US film critic Roger Ebert as one of his Top 100 Great Movies.

EXO is a Korean and Chinese boy band known for their tight choreography and glitzy live shows. In the spring of 2017, they plan to launch a sub-unit, EXO-CBX, comprising three members of the original group, Chen, Baekhyun, and Xiumin. EXO regularly performs across Asia and has been among the top-grossing K-pop acts of the last several years.

BTS, also known as the Bangtan Boys, are a seven-member boy band, who in 2016 set a US record for becoming the best-selling and highest-charting K-pop act in the United States when their album *Wings* debuted at number 26 on the Billboard 200. Despite having no songs in the English, the group sold out two US tours and remains a favorite among K-pops acts to achieve breakthrough success in the elusive North American market. Unlike most other K-pop groups, BTS write most of their own songs, which feature socially conscious lyrics.

Suzy (Korean name Bae Suji) is a singer and actress who has been a fixture of many TV shows and series. In 2016 she starred in the drama *Uncontrollably Fond*, which garnered her many news fans across Asia and earned her the distinction of being the first female Korean celebrity honored with a likeness at Madame Tussaud's Wax Museum in Hong Kong.

Song Hye-kyo is an actress whose role in the television drama *Autumn in My Heart* established her as one of the first Hallyu stars. In Korea, her work in the drama *All In* gained her further fame and recognition. More recently, she starred in the popular drama *Descendants of the Sun* alongside Song Joong-ki.

Girls' Generation is an 8-member pop group whose songs like "I Got a Boy" and "Gee" earned them immense popularity in Korea, as well as in neighbouring Japan, where they regularly sell out concert tours and claim legions of adoring fans. Their smiling faces can also be found on advertisements for a range of products from perfume to fried chicken. In 2012, three of the members, Taeyeon, Tiffany, and Seohyun broke off to form a sub-group called TTS, though Taeyeon and Tiffany have since embarked on solo careers. The main group continues to perform, and in March 2017, they celebrated their 10th anniversary—a remarkable achievement in a crowded field of aspiring K-pop groups and a testament to their enduring popularity in South Korea and beyond.

Park Jin-young is a singer/songwriter turned music producer, whose production company JYP Entertainment has spawned many popular K-pop acts. He is also a judge on the reality show *K-Pop Star*, which for several seasons has auditioned and previewed hundreds of aspiring performers from around the world.

Gang-Ho-dong is a former traditional Korean wrestler who for nearly two decades has been a fixture on Korean television as the comedic host of a variety of shows. Recognisable by his large stature, crew cut and booming voice, Gang can these days be seen on *New Journey to the West*, a reality travel show.

Yoo Jae-suk is a TV personality, comedian and host who has been a mainstay of Korean television for over a decade. The quick-witted Yoo has featured in popular programmes like *Happy Together*, *Infinite Challenge* and *Running Man*, and enjoys such broad popularity that he has been dubbed "The Nation's MC".

Sports

Oh Seung-hwan is a professional baseball player, who starred as a relief pitcher in the KBO for several seasons before making the jump to the MLB, where he currently plays for the Saint Louis Cardinals. Known by Korean and American fans as the "Final Boss" for his tendency to successfully hold late leads, he has also been dubbed the "Stone Buddha" in reference to his composure in the high-pressure role of closing pitcher.

Kim Yuna is a South Korean figure skater with 11 current or former world records and wall full of medals to her credit: she was a gold medalist in the 2010 Olympics and a silver medalist in 2014, and has won or placed in every other major international tournament, a blizzard of achievements that has earned her the nickname "Queen Yuna" in South Korea. Kim retired from skating in 2014, and in 2016 was formally inducted into South Korea's sports Hall of Fame.

Ki Sung-yueng is a soccer player who plays midfield for Swansea City in the English Premier League, and is the current captain of the South Korean national team. Since

2007, Ki has earned over 70 caps playing for South Korea, and has appeared in two FIFA World Cups, two AFC Asian Cups, and the 2012 Olympics, where he and the other members of the "Red Devils" earned a bronze medal. In 2013, Ki married the actress **Han Hye-jin**, and in 2015, the couple celebrated the birth of their daughter, Si-on.

Business

Chung Mong-koo is the chairman of Hyundai Motor Group, one of the largest conglomerates (or chaebol) in Korea. Chung is the second son of the company's founder, **Chung Ju-yung**, who handed control of the conglomerate to his son just prior to his death in 2001. In 2007, Chung was convicted of embezzlement but was pardoned the following year by President **Lee Myoung-bak**. At 79 years old, Chung still rises early and actively manages the company, though it is expected that he will one day hand the reins of leadership to his son and heir-apparent, **Chung Eui-sun**.

Lee Kun-hee is chairman of the Samsung group, Korea's largest conglomerate, a position he has held since the 1987 death of his father, Samsung founder **Lee Byung-chul**. Lee is one of Korea's wealthiest men, and in 2014 was ranked by Forbes Magazine as the 35th most powerful person in the world. His son, **Lee Jae-yong**, the vice-chairman of the Samsung group, was arrested in February 2017 on charges of embezzlement, bribery and perjury, and at press time was standing trial. It remains to be seen how this will affect his prospects as the heir to the chairmanship; the current turmoil has even fired speculation that should vice-chairman Lee be obliged to step down, his sister **Lee Boo-jin** may someday step into the leadership role.

CULTURE QUIZ

SITUATION 1

You are having a few drinks with a same-sex Korean friend. At some point in the evening, you find that his or her hand is resting on your thigh. What should you do?

Ⓐ Brush the hand away, while making it clear that your friend is misinterpreting the nature of your relationship.

Ⓑ Accept it, and pay it no mind.

Ⓒ Place your own hand on your friend's thigh.

Ⓓ Tell your friend that it makes you uncomfortable because it's not customary for friends to do that where you come from.

Comments

Because same-sex Korean friends are much more touchy-feely than the average Westerner, answer Ⓐ would almost certainly be an overreaction. If you are comfortable in doing so, answers Ⓒ or Ⓑ would be fine, though it's also ok to ask someone not to do that (Choice Ⓓ) if it makes you uncomfortable, even if you understand the intent.

SITUATION 2

Your apartment security guard has been very helpful and friendly throughout the year, so you think to get him a small gift for the Lunar New Year Holiday. When the day comes, you hand him a bottle of whiskey, but he expresses surprise and says he cannot accept it. What should you do?

Ⓐ Continue offering it to him until he accepts it.

Ⓑ Because he is just performing his duty, he considers a gift unwarranted. Withdraw the offer, and you might even apologise for inadvertently insulting him.

ⓒ Immediately withdraw the offer, because you are breaking the law by offering him a gift.

ⓓ Assume that he is a teetotaller, and exchange the gift for something more suitable (a box of tropical fruit, a good ball-point pen, etc).

Comments

There is no law that forbids giving a gift to people like apartment staff, housekeepers, or other non-public workers who work for you in some capacity. Not everyone offers gifts to security guards, so he may in fact not be expecting one, but many people do give such gifts at the end of the year, and such gifts are generally appreciated. Being a teetotaller would not be sufficient reason to refuse the gift, as pointing that out might cause the gift-giver embarrassment and would show a lack of tact or gratitude. Many people will however initially refuse a gift in a ritual show of humility or to not appear greedy, but they will gratefully accept it on the second or third attempt, thus, the best answer is **ⓐ**.

SITUATION 3

A co-worker tells you on Thursday about the upcoming First Birthday Party (*ddol janchi*) being held for the child of another co-worker acquaintance this coming Saturday, and she invites you to come along. What should you do?

ⓐ Skip the party, because you weren't invited by the host.

ⓑ Track down the host, and confirm that you are welcome to attend.

ⓒ Consider the party optional, but don't go out of your way to attend.

ⓓ Do your best to at least make an appearance at the birthday party.

Comments

Many events, even relatively formal ones like a *ddol janchi*, may be planned late, and guests are often invited by word of mouth. In the case of a *ddol janchi*, wedding, or funeral, all co-workers can assume they are invited, so choices **Ⓐ** and **Ⓑ** can be ruled out, as there is no reason to assume you would be unwelcome. Strictly speaking, your attendance is optional, but because it is an honour to attend, and is also an excellent way to build and deepen bonds with the people in your social and professional networks, you should consider dropping whatever else you had planned that day and try to make it.

SITUATION 4

You are out for dinner with some Korean colleagues, and your server places several bottles of beer and glasses on the table. One colleague hands you a glass. What do you do?

Ⓐ Use the glass if you want, but feel free to drink from one of the bottles (assuming there is at least one for everyone).

Ⓑ Hold the glass while your colleague fills it, then hand him or her a glass and do the same.

Ⓒ Pass the glass to whoever doesn't have one.

Ⓓ Fill your glass, and those of all the other members of your group.

Comments

One never fills one's own glass, so **Ⓓ** can be ruled out straight away. These days, drinking from one's own bottle in a bar or pub is common, but drinking from a bottle in a situation where several bottles have been ordered for a group would strike a Korean observer as odd. If there are other people at the table who don't yet have glasses, passing them until everyone has a glass is good form, but at some point, when the last glass is handed to you, be ready to receive a pour with two hands, and be ready to fill your colleague's glass in like manner once yours is full.

SITUATION 5

You are introduced to a new colleague, who gives his Korean name, and adds that his English nickname is Danny. How should you address him?

Ⓐ Feel free to address him by his nickname in one-on-one settings, but be prepared to address him or refer to him more formally in group settings.

Ⓑ Use the nickname in any setting, but only if you can confirm that he is the same age or younger than you.

Ⓒ Ignore the nickname, and either use his surname plus job title plus –*nim* if he is senior to you, or use his given name plus –*ssi* if younger or junior to you.

Comments

Many Koreans, especially those with unusual or hard-to-pronounce names, adopt nicknames to make things easier on their foreign colleagues and friends. In the case above, mentioning his nickname while being introduced may be considered an invitation to use it, whatever his age relative to yours. If you feel uncomfortable or strange doing that (because for example he is older than you), there is no harm in addressing him more formally, as in choice **Ⓒ**. If you do use the nickname, it's still considered polite to use the more formal style of address in group settings or when speaking about him to a third person, so **Ⓐ** would be acceptable, but **Ⓑ** would not be a safe choice.

DOS AND DON'TS

DOS

- Use two hands when giving or receiving something from someone senior to you.
- Take off your shoes when entering someone's home.
- Learn titles of those senior to you and use them when addressing them.
- Refer to the Sea of Japan as the East Sea.
- Dress formally in work settings.
- Show commitment to your company, school or organisation.
- Double-check large numbers.
- Pour drinks for others, not for yourself.
- Cultivate relationships with Koreans.
- Make an effort to learn Korean, and to alter your English for maximum clarity.
- Carry a good supply of business cards, and receive them properly from others.

DON'TS

- Address seniors by their first names.
- Start eating before the eldest person begins.
- Show anger.
- Openly disagree with or contradict someone senior to you in a public setting.
- Bow out of company dinners or outings if you can help it.
- Assume your cultural norms and values are universal or are prioritised the same way.
- Use your index finger to point at someone.
- Engage in public displays of affection.
- Read too much into a lack of eye contact.
- Write someone's name in red ink.

GLOSSARY

PEOPLE

Agassi	Unmarried woman
Ajeossi	Married man
Ajumma	Married woman
Chingu	Friend
Gyeongbi ajeossi	Apartment security guard
Haksaeng	Student
Hyoung(nim)	Term of respect for older brother or male friend
Imo	Polite but familiar term of address for an older married women
Mudang	Shaman (female)
Sajang(nim)	Manager
Seonsaengnim	Teacher (respectful term of address)
Waegukin	Foreigner
Wangtta	Outcast, pariah

PLACES

Hagwon	Private academy
Hanok jip	Traditional Korean house
Jjimjilbang	Sauna
Minbak	Type of accommodation similar to a B&B
Mogyoktang	Bathhouse
Noraebang	"Singing room"
Officetel	A type of small apartment

Pojang macha	Tent-covered street cart that serves alcohol and side dishes
Yeogwan	Accommodation similar to a motel

THINGS

Anju	Any type of side dish served with alcohol
Banchan	Side dishes served with a meal
Banmal	Informal Korean speech
Bap	Cooked white rice
Charye	Ancestral memorial rites held on major holidays (Chuseok, Seollal)
Chaebol	Conglomerate
Chuseok	Major Korean fall holiday
Hanbok	Traditional Korean clothing
Hangeul	The Korean writing system
Hallyu	The Korean Wave, refers to the promotion and spread of Korean culture worldwide
Hwaesik	Company or staff dinner
Jesa (or gijesa)	Ancestral memorial rite held on the anniversary of a parent or grandparent's death
Jeon	A type of savory pancake
Jeonsae	A rental system involving a large initial deposit and little or no monthly rent
Jondaetmal	Formal (polite) Korean speech
Kimchi	A class of fermented vegetables, the best known of which is cabbage (*baechu*) kimchi

Kimjang (or gimjang)	The process of making kimchi, usually in late fall
Makkeoli	A type of cloudy rice wine
Poktanju	Soju boilermaker
Pyoung	Unit of area measurement roughly equal to 3.3 square meters
Suneung	University entrance exam
Seollal	Lunar New Year holiday
Soju	A type of clear liquor
Wolsae	A system of monthly rent

ACRONYMS AND ABBREVIATIONS

BIFF	The Busan International Film Festival
DMZ	The Demilitarized Zone, which forms the border between North and South Korea
DPRK	The Democratic People's Republic of Korea (North Korea)
KOICA	Korea International Cooperation Agency
OECD	The Organization for Economic Cooperation and Development
ROK	The Republic of Korea (South Korea)
SKY	Shorthand for three of the top universities in Korea (Seoul National University, Korea University, Yonsei University)

USEFUL EXPRESSIONS

Bangapseumnida.	Nice to meet you.
Annyeong haseyo?	Common, polite greeting. Literally "Are you at peace?"
Annyeong hasimnikka?	More formal greeting. Same meaning as above.
Annyeong.	Informal greeting/farewell used for friends or children.
Annyeonghi gaseyo.	Goodbye (to the person who is leaving)
Annyeonghi gyeseyo.	Goodbye (to the person who is staying)
Yeogiyo!	"Here, please!"; used to summon restaurant servers or bar staff, or to get someone's attention in public.
Jamgganmanyo.	"Just a moment, please." This is also roughly equivalent to "Pardon me" when for example making your way through a crowded space.
Jwesonghamnida	"Excuse me" (Not used for interrupting but for pardoning yourself when you have for example bumped into someone.)
Mianhamnida	"I'm sorry."
Geonbae!	Bottom's up! (literally "empty glass")
Masitgae deusaeyo!	Bon appétit!
Chal meokgaesseumnida	Literally "I will eat well"; said in response to "Masitgae dusaeyo"
Chal meogeosseumnida	"I ate well"; said after the bill has been paid

Gamsa hamnida / *Gomapsumnida*	Thank you
___-ga juseyo	[To a taxi driver] "Please go to ___"
Yeogi naeryeojuseyo.	"Please let me off here."
Igeo eolmayeyo?	"How much does this cost?"
Yeongeo hal jul arayo?	Do you speak English?
Hwajangsil eodiyeyo?	Where is the toilet?

RESOURCE GUIDE

IMPORTANT TELEPHONE NUMBERS
- Police   112
- Fire/Ambulance   119
- Directory Assistance   114
- Tourism and Translation Service   1330
- Emergency Medical Information   02-1339
- Seoul Dasan Call Center   120

  (For information on Seoul government services, restaurants, transportation, legal counseling, tourism, schools, and more)

- Korea Immigration Service   1345
- Government Call Center   110

  (For information on government policy)

HOSPITALS

Most hospitals around Korea have English-speaking staff to assist you, but the following hospitals have international clinics geared toward foreigners.

Seoul
- Asan Medical Center
  02-3010-5001-5003
- Cheil Hospital and Women's Health Center
  02-2000-7437
- Hanyang University Hospital
  02-2290-9553
- Samsung Medical Center
  02-3410-0200/0226
- Seoul National University Hospital
  02-2072-0505

- **Yonsei Severance Hospital**
  02-2228-5800

Busan
- **Inje University Haeundae Paik Hospital**
  051-797-0566
- **Pusan National University Hospital**
  051-240-7472-3

Daegu
- **Daegu Fatima Hospital**
  053-940-7114
- **Keimyung University Dongsan Medical Center**
  053-250-7303 or 018-564-7371 (24 hours)
- **Yeungnam University Medical Center**
  053-623-4114 or 010-4786-8001 (24 hours)

EMBASSIES

There are 136 foreign embassies and consulates in Korea. A full list with contact information can be found at www. embassy.goabroad.com/embassies-in/south-korea
- **United States Embassy (Seoul)**
  02-397-4114
  United States Consulate (Busan)
  051–863-0731/2
- **U.K. Embassy (Seoul)**
  02-3210-5500
  U.K. Consulate (Busan)
  051-463-4630 and 070-8862-4100

- **Canadian Embassy (Seoul)**
  02-3783-6000
  Canadian Consulate (Busan)
  051-204-5581
- **Australian Embassy (Seoul)**
  02-2003-0100
  Australian Consulate (Busan)
  051-647-1762
- **New Zealand Embassy (Seoul)**
  02-3701-7700
  New Zealand Consulate (Busan)
  051-600-3350
- **Embassy of Ireland (Seoul)**
  02-774-6455/7
- **South African Embassy (Seoul)**
  02-792-4855

RELIGIOUS INSTITUTIONS

South Korea has a large variety of religious institutions that welcome foreigners and have services in English. An exhaustive list is not possible here, but can be found at www.korea4expats.com.

VOLUNTEER ORGANISATIONS

Googling "Korea Volunteer" turns up a number of NGOs and charitable organisations in Korea that are always looking for help with a variety of initiatives, including teaching English to orphans, North Korean refugees, the disadvantaged, and the elderly; feeding the homeless; fostering shelter animals and fighting animal abuse; campaigning for human rights, and many others.

CHAMBERS OF COMMERCE

- **United States (AMCHAM)**
  02-564-2040
- **Britain (BCCK)**
  02-720-9406
- **Canada (CanCham)**
  02-554-0245
- **Australia (AustCham)**
  02-2010-8831/2
- **New Zealand (Kiwi Chamber)**
  02-725-3905
- **Europe (ECCK)**
  02-6261-2716

OTHER GROUPS AND ORGANISATIONS

- **Alcoholics Anonymous**
  www.aainkorea.org
- **International Spouses of Koreans Association**
  www.iskaonline.com
- **KOTESOL** (professional organisation for teachers of English)
  www.kotesol.org
- **Royal Asiatic Society Korea Branch**
  02-763-9483
- **Seoul Foreign Correspondents' Club**
  www.sfcc.or.kr
- **Lion's Club International**

NEWSPAPERS AND MAGAZINES

South Korea is served by several English language periodicals, most of them taking Seoul as their base and focus. Magazines like *10 Magazine*, *Groove Korea*, and *Seoul Magazine* are available at many locations around Seoul.

Busan is served by the online magazine *BusanHaps.com*. For print newspapers, check out *The Korea Times, The Korea Herald*, and *The Korea Joongang Daily* (which comes bundled with *The International Herald Tribune*). There are also a few English-language online newspapers, like *The Hankyoreh, Digital Chosun Ilbo, Dong-a Ilbo*, and *Yonhap News*.

ONLINE RESOURCES

- **Talk to Me in Korean**
  Popular and well-produced YouTube channel offering free lessons in Korean.

- **Ask a Korean** (www.askakorean.blogspot.kr)
  An excellent, long-running blog by a US-based Korean who fields both common and not-so-common questions from readers.

- **Korea4expats.com**
  Comprehensive site geared toward people who are living and working in Korea.

- **Korea Tourism Organization Official Website**
  (www.English.visitkorea.or.kr)
  English language information, on travel, shopping, accommodation, and things to do around Korea.

- **Whatthebook.com**
  What the Book? is the largest English-language bookstore in Korea, located in Seoul's Itaewon district. Ships anywhere in Korea.

- **G-Market** (global.gmarket.co.kr)
  The biggest online shopping mall in Korea. Fairly easy to navigate for English speakers.

- **Askajumma.com**
  An online concierge service that can order you anything from concert tickets to pizza.

FURTHER READING

Coyner, Thomas L. *Doing Business in Korea*. Seoul: Seoul Selection, 2010.

Crane, Paul S. *Korean Patterns*. Seoul: Royal Asiatic Society, 1978.

Halberstam, David. *The Coldest Winter: America and the Korean War*. New York: Hyperion, 2007.

Hong, Euny. *The Birth of Korean Cool: How One Nation Is Conquering the World Through Pop Culture*. New York: Picador, 2014.

Oberdorfer, Dan. *The Two Koreas: A Contemporary History*. New York: Basic Books, 1997.

Revere, Stephen. *Survival Korean*. Seoul: Nexus, 2015.

Rhie, Wonbok. *Korea Unmasked*. Seoul: Gimm-Young International, 2005.

Tudor, Daniel. *Korea: The Impossible Country*. Singapore: Tuttle Publishing, 2012.

ABOUT THE
AUTHOR

 **John Bocskay** hails from Westchester County, New York and has been writing and teaching in South Korea since 1998. He lives in Busan with his wife Aeran, and his daughters Cheyoon, Cheyoung and Chewon. John writes a column on expatriate life and Korean culture for *Busan Haps Magazine*, and his other work has appeared in *The Korea Times*, *Stripes Korea*, *The Kukje Shinmun*, and *Branding in Asia Magazine*.

Follow him on facebook@johnnicholasbocskay.

INDEX

Titles in the **CultureShock!** series:

Argentina	France	Philippines
Australia	Germany	Portugal
Austria	Great Britain	Russia
Bahrain	Greece	San Francisco
Bali	Hawaii	Saudi Arabia
Beijing	Hong Kong	Scotland
Belgium	Hungary	Sri Lanka
Berlin	India	Shanghai
Bolivia	Ireland	Singapore
Borneo	Italy	South Africa
Bulgaria	Jakarta	Spain
Brazil	Japan	Sri Lanka
Cambodia	Korea	Sweden
Canada	Laos	Switzerland
Chicago	London	Syria
Chile	Malaysia	Taiwan
China	Mauritius	Thailand
Costa Rica	Morocco	Tokyo
Cuba	Munich	Travel Safe
Czech Republic	Myanmar	Turkey
Denmark	Netherlands	United Arab Emirates
Dubai	New Zealand	USA
Ecuador	Norway	Vancouver
Egypt	Pakistan	Venezuela
Finland	Paris	Vietnam

For more information about any of these titles, please contact the Publisher via email at: genref@sg.marshallcavendish.com or visit our website at: www.marshallcavendish.com/genref